To my husband, John, whose love and encouragement
undergird all my work

Contents

★ hitherto unpublished work

★ hitherto unpublished work

Acknowledgements

I would like to thank the following:

The British Library for their kind permission to print selections from *Commentaries of Heaven*.

The Folger Library, Washington DC, for their kind permission to print part of *The Ceremonial Law*.

The Lambeth Palace Library for their kind permission to print selections from *The Kingdom of God* and *Love*.

Donald Allchin, Cal McFarlane, David Scott and Bishop Geoffrey Rowell for their help on the way, as well as Bishop Kenneth Stevenson and Sarah for making their home a centre for discussion and a place where friendships could be forged. I would like to thank, in addition, Colin Sydenham who shared his Latin expertise.

I would also like to thank Elizabeth Marsh of SPCK for commissioning this book and guiding me through the process of publication.

The Golden Age of Spiritual Writing

The Golden Age of Spiritual Writing brings together a series of books of English 'spiritual' poetry and prose, selected and introduced by well-known contemporary authors and scholars. Many of the writers on whom this series focuses flourished during the seventeenth century. You may well ask, 'Why concentrate on writers of the seventeenth century? Wasn't it a long time ago?' Historically, that period might well seem 'a long time ago', especially when we consider the huge changes in communications and in scientific understanding, and, yet, looked at with the long view of human history, the seventeenth century is quite recent. It was, in many ways, the beginning of the modern age. We share with the people of that time the struggles and strains of being human, the joys as well as the challenges of the natural world, and the seemingly incontrovertible facts of birth and death. In our religious lives, too, we want to talk about the challenges of new cultures bearing down on what we consider eternal truths, and the relationship between different Christian traditions.

But we do bother about the seventeenth-century writers, and have done with increasing enthusiasm since the early part of the twentieth century, with the name and influence of T. S. Eliot ranking large. I think we bother about them for three main reasons. First, they write well. Second, they tell eternal truths. And third, for our spiritually bewildered age, they fill a dry well with clear, fresh water.

There is something about the English language of this period that has an element of the miraculous. We find this most commonly in the plays of Shakespeare and in the Authorized Version of the Bible: the two books without which any stay on a desert island is deficient. Their language is not so removed from our own that we are utterly confused by it, but it is freshly coined enough to retain its life, its bite and chew. It has the power to evoke in us, physically, the moods, emotions and thoughts the words are trying to express. The words and the rhythms can make us cry and laugh and ponder with a huge intensity. Someone could probably explain this miracle and find it, for sure, in other writers of different ages, but all I want to do is to encourage readers to see if it is true for them about the seventeenth century. However, when it comes to dealing with the translated material of Lancelot Andrewes then different linguistic criteria have to be applied.

The words have to be about something. It is not just a matter of style or sound. The words have to tell us something that we find valuable. This series concentrates on spiritual writers. Each of them refers easily and unashamedly to God, and not infrequently to Jesus Christ as the revelation of God's love in and for the world. They write of sin and prayer, of salvation and love, of death and heaven and hell, and they mean real things by them. The writers precede the growth of rationalism that developed in the eighteenth century. Are we not too grown up and too clever for such things? Are we not, as Eliot put it, banging an antique drum? Each of the books in this series will be at pains to persuade us that this is not so, and more importantly, the writers themselves will do so, too. They take the great spiritual themes of all times and places: desire, fear, decision-making, a sense of wonder and of awe, anxiety and loss, and, by their own vision and breadth of experience, make them reach down to us in our own day.

Reading the great classics of spiritual literature of whatever age today will always be a new thing, it is a new generation that is reading them. Reading Traherne in an era of massive pollution will put his sense of wonder and affection for the natural world in a new political context. Donne's honesty about sex and religion will raise questions about the nature of humanity, which, after Freud, will seem as real as ever. Herbert's gentle, pragmatic ethics might encourage a new generation to reflect on standards of behaviour and the place of an ordered life in a free-floating world. Each of the writers presented in this series will have something to contribute to the contemporary debate. Pondering these questions will be to the benefit of both writer and reader. The echoes of great literature come not only from within the text itself, but also from outside the text. In reading the poetry, the thoughts, the prayers, we make them live again. For people searching for the words that express what they want to say, here in this series will be some familiar resources and, I trust, some revelations.

As editor of the series, I would like to thank all the authors who agreed to contribute. I am especially grateful for the high quality of their work, which has made my task so much easier. I have worked closely throughout with the editorial team at SPCK, especially with Liz Marsh. I am immensely grateful to them for their friendly support and for their decision to take on the publication of this fascinating area of spiritual writing. Without them this series would never have come together.

David Scott
Winchester

Introduction

The Traherne I first met was a largely discredited one. A 'minor' poet of the seventeenth century, present in my undergraduate seventeenth century anthology, though entirely squeezed out of others. What a terrible fate to be a minor poet, I thought. I could see the inferiority of his rhymes – certainly all the critics could, and who was I to argue with such an august company? But despite his relegation to the second division there was something in his poetry and in his prose meditations that sang. Above the struggle and satisfaction of Herbert and the passionate turmoil of Donne, the contrasting light and shade of Vaughan, unlike any of the other metaphysical poets with whom he was grouped, this singular voice rose confident and queer, calling with breathless elation. And I felt, even then, that there was more to him than had met the corporate eye. I discovered that if you can invoke all the powers of your imagination to follow him he will take you on ventures into time and eternity that none of the others will. He will turn your understanding inside out, thrill, surprise and exhaust you.

But there was something else in Traherne that challenged my thinking. I met him in the literature classes of an evangelical Christian liberal arts college in America, a place where the orthodoxy of the writer mattered, and yet he seemed to teeter precariously on the edges of orthodoxy. I met him in a country in which church and state are held to be strictly separate affairs – and he so convinced of the interconnectedness of both. But perhaps most profoundly I came convinced of my natural depravity, born a sinner in a world full of sin, and found in him glimpses of glory. I do not mean by this mere optimism, nor do I mean a kind of pre-romantic nature-loving positivism. What I found in Traherne was grace. Unimaginable divine generosity woven into the very fabric of the universe. And that vision of a gracious God and his bountiful creation has whispered hopefully to me ever since.

Biography

Traherne's life remains something of a sketch: a few clear strokes mark the boundaries – his education, his ordination, his death – with other lines added and sometimes rubbed out again and redrawn. We have the dates of his entry to Brasenose College, Oxford, in 1652 and of his BA in 1656 and MA in 1661, a record of his appointment to Credenhill, a rural parish in Herefordshire, in 1657; and of his ordination in 1660. We know that he became chaplain to Sir Orlando Bridgeman, Lord Keeper of the Seal, in 1669, and that he died in Bridgeman's household at Teddington in the first week in October 1674 at the young age of 38. We know something of what he was like as a person from the little asides he makes in his writing – that he talked too much, that he was passionate in his beliefs and could argue his point tenaciously, that he sometimes found the work of loving people in his parish exhausting. We may deduce something of his nature from his prodigious output. And we have the record of his will in which he gave his books and his best hat to his brother Philip and his second best hat to his servant. The several houses he had owned in Hereford became almshouses for the poor of that city. It would seem that he tried to live by his own motto from the fourth *Century*: 'He lives most like an Angel that lives upon least Himself, and doth most Good to others.'

But the early picture of an impoverished and possibly orphaned Traherne who spent most of his days as an isolated rector is being redrafted. Anthony à Wood describes Traherne as 'a shoemaker's son of Hereford'. But the gossip writer John Aubrey's account of Traherne's night encounter with an apparition records several apprentices sleeping in the household. Traherne's father may have been not so much a simple cobbler as the master of a small cottage industry; and it is possible that Traherne's early childhood was spent not in penury but as a member of the new rising middle class.

Traherne is very much connected with Hereford. He is thought to have been born there and is very likely related to a well-to-do family of Trahernes who lived in nearby Lugwardine, several miles to the north-east, as well as to an elder Philip

Traherne, twice mayor of Hereford.[1] His connection to the nearby parish of Credenhill extended over his whole working lifetime. He was resident there even after he became Bridgeman's chaplain, and it may be that he never lived in Bridgeman's London home at all, but moved to the household in 1673–74, only after Bridgeman's removal to Teddington. As late as 1673 his church-warden at Credenhill wrote: 'Our minister is continually resident amongst us.' As his biographer Julia Smith notes, his church-wardens describe him as 'a good & godly man, well learned . . . a good liver' who 'visited the poor and instructed the youth'.[2] He continued to hold the living until his death. This is not to say that he was intellectually or socially isolated. He enjoyed the fellowship of several Oxford-educated local clergy and was connected with eminent families in the county. He worked closely with the Hereford Cathedral clergy: in 1671 and 1672 he acted for the Dean of Hereford's consistory court, and on his death was described by one of the canons as 'one of the most pious & ingenious men' he had known. It may well be that his trips to Oxford and London were supplemented by regular use of the Hereford Cathedral library. Certainly, Traherne was no simple child of the English–Welsh border, warbling his mystical songs to the rural air. His own prodigious achievements, his education and his con-nections all point to a man as much at home in the university and in the capital as in the country. Nevertheless, he is rooted in Hereford; it was his childhood home, the region in which he obtained his first living, and the place to which his earthly assets were disposed upon his death.

Discovery of Works

The story of the discovery of Traherne's work is one of the most fascinating in English literature. It is a tale of chance and mishap, of scholarly commitment and of serendipity that runs over centuries. For of all of Traherne's prolific work, only *Roman Forgeries* (1673) was published in his lifetime. *Christian Ethicks*, prepared by Traherne for publication, was published posthumously in 1675, just one year after his death. These theological works were largely appreciated and admired in their day, but on their

day, but on their own they were not enough to establish
Traherne as a writer of continuing interest for readers of
subsequent centuries, and Traherne might have disappeared from
literary and theological view were it not for much later
discoveries. There were intermediate publications. The
Thanksgivings were published as *A Serious and Pathetical
Contemplation* in 1699, but this publication was anonymous.
Traherne's *Thanksgivings*, the *Hexameron* and his *Meditations and
Devotions* were also published in various forms under differing
titles between 1673 and 1717, but these publications were
incomplete and possibly misattributed to Susanna Hopton.
Traherne's voice seemed to have fallen silent. And it was not
until nearly 200 years later, at the turn of the twentieth century
when major discoveries began to occur, that Traherne suddenly
became a writer who sparked a flurry of interest, though,
interestingly, this time not as a theologian but as a poet. For the
anonymous manuscripts that were discovered by an amateur
booklover, William Brooke, as he rummaged in the bargain
baskets of two separate booksellers in London in the winter of
1896-97 turned out to be the manuscripts of some of Traherne's
poems and of the *Centuries of Meditations*, or *Centuries* as they are
commonly called.

Brooke bought these interesting and neglected manuscripts for
a few pence and sold them on to a well-known collector who
mistook them for Vaughan's and was just about to publish them
under Vaughan's name when (conveniently for Traherne) he
suddenly died. Bertram Dobell purchased these from the deceased
collector's library and, discovering, eventually, a poem in *Christian
Ethicks* to be identical with one in one of the manuscripts, found
incontrovertible evidence of Traherne's authorship. It was Dobell
who published *The Poetical Works* in 1903 and who, in his
prefatory notes, introduced Traherne to the literary world as their
new 'Poet of Felicity'.

Nearly 60 years later, an obscure manuscript described by a
Birmingham bookseller simply as 'Select Meditations. Four
Centuries' was identified as Traherne's. This small leather-bound
volume had been badly mutilated; most of the first *Century* was

missing, and a number of other pages had been removed. Nothing is known of its whereabouts during the 290 years between Traherne's death in 1674 and its discovery in 1964. Written in several hands, the manuscript is a copy although it shows no sign of being prepared for publication and it may be that *Select Meditations* was written for Traherne's own friends.[3] It was not published until 1997.

Commentaries of Heaven, however, written 'For the Satisfaction of Atheists, & the Consolation of Christians', was intended for a wider audience, though it was saved from oblivion by only two people. For this manuscript was rescued, amazingly, from the top of a smouldering rubbish heap in the mid-1960s by a Mr and Mrs Wookey of Lancashire, the leather covers already alight. Taken among their household things when they moved to Toronto, Canada, it was not identified until 1981. Despite its dance with destruction, it is one of the most well-preserved of all of the Traherne manuscripts. Loose notes for the manuscript have survived, in two cases with the seventeenth-century pins by which they were attached still intact.

In 1997, almost 100 years after the discovery of the first unpublished manuscripts in those two London book barrows, two more autograph manuscripts came to light in two different libraries, in two different countries. While, at the Folger Library in Washington DC, Julia Smith and Laetitia Yeandle were discovering *The Ceremonial Law*, an unfinished poem – 1,800 lines of heroic couplets – based on the books of Genesis and Exodus, across an ocean another discovery was about to take place. On a wet winter day early in 1997, the late Jeremy Maule, Fellow of Trinity College, Cambridge, driven by the bad weather and his passion for manuscripts, sought refuge in the library at Lambeth Palace in London. Here, while perusing a catalogue that listed and described some unidentified manuscripts, he happened upon the phrase 'Seeds of Eternity'. His interest was seized; he summoned the manuscript and was amazed to discover its pages covered in the tiny writing of Traherne.

The story of the discovery of Traherne manuscripts is, tantalizingly, a story without a clear end. What new manuscripts remain to be discovered and how these may affect our reading of Traherne we do not know. But we may be sure that new readings will emerge. One of the very exciting things about this anthology is that alongside the familiar texts it also publishes for the first time some of the newest discoveries.

Literary Critique

The literary critique of Traherne, begun early in the twentieth century, and based on discoveries we now know to be partial, is a somewhat lopsided beast. On the publication of the *Centuries* and the Dobell poems, Traherne was hailed as a 'new poet', and readers of the newly published Dobell poems were promised that this new light that had lain for so long in obscurity was 'destined to shine with undiminished lustre' as long as the English tongue should endure. Enthusiasm for his lyric verse sparked a whole new readership while his previous theological works, already forgotten, were largely ignored by the emerging criticism. Traherne the theologian (as he was in his own day) was replaced by Traherne the poet. For more than half a century Traherne was seen in this light as a nature-loving ruralist whose vision of childhood innocence informed his optimistic view of life, a simple soul – the 'Poet of Felicity'. However, by the mid-twentieth century this first burst of enthusiasm for his verse waned and preference gradually shifted to his prose, particularly the *Centuries*. Marked as they are by an instinctive rhythmical sense often lacking in his poetry, the *Centuries* became and remain his most highly acclaimed work. For in the *Centuries* mid-twentieth-century readers found his themes of early innocence and enjoyment of the world, the search for felicity and the soul's stretch toward the infinite reiterated with the same passionate fervour of thought but with clearer diction.

'An Empty Book is like an Infants Soul, in which any Thing may be Written' became a catchphrase of his early innocence. Passages such as 'The corn was Orient and Immortal Wheat, which never should be reaped, nor was ever sown' from the third *Century* seemed to encapsulate the glory of his childhood vision. 'The Infinity of God is our Enjoyment' he wrote with utter certainty. Still, his readers were sometimes frustrated. His passion for the created world was inspiring; his forays into the infinite and the abstract thrilled. Yet none of his works seemed to ground him in the ordinary stuff of life. The historical and intellectual events of his day seemed largely unrepresented in his work. Christian theologians found in him no need of grace and an avoidance of the muck of sin and its flood of forgiveness, the terrible weight of guilt or the dark night of the soul. The discoveries of the late twentieth century, with their nuances of struggle and of grace, the *Select Meditations*, the *Commentaries of Heaven*, *The Ceremonial Law* and all of the Lambeth manuscript works were as yet unidentified. And so the Traherne that emerged was a Traherne with neither context nor intellectual system, unconnected to both the theology and the history of his day, not quite orthodox, adrift in some imaginary land of optimism and good will, proclaiming a gospel of reinstated innocence and enjoyment of the world.

As one modern critic has ably stated,

> To read through the criticism that has so far been written on him is to discover a Traherne who is distinguished from his seventeenth-century peers by the fact that he is blissfully untroubled by the tensions, doubts, and anxieties that (we are repeatedly told) mark the age in general.

and 'If Traherne had nothing to say to his own age and time, what can he have to say to ours?'[4] It is true that there is something, if not alienated, at least other-worldly in Traherne. He speaks of a world most of us only remember as if it were his present and his future. And that is more than part of his charm; it is his constant vision. Another world is his origin and his destination. Another world behind, in, under, above, beneath this one from which we are separated by the merest veil and yet to which we are invited by the faintest piercing birdsong and the greatest human act alike. For Traherne this world is a gateway to heaven, this world not avoided but transfigured; and so it is not so much that he shuns looking at, but that he is busy looking under. He is simply engaged in the act of finding meaning. This meaning is not only to be found in the natural world, for the wealth of insights the newest discoveries afford confirm his place in an intellectual and social world as well. And as modern scholarship applies itself to these texts, a hitherto 'alienated' Traherne is being replaced by a more integrated Traherne. Traherne the naive woodland warbler sequestered away in his country parish becomes Traherne the public priest and private chaplain, a scholar and theologian more concerned with the theological and political struggles of his day than we had ever imagined.

Sources and Influences

Traherne's sources are wide-ranging and eclectic enough to make him seem at a glance intellectually promiscuous, a magpie who picks up bright bits from one source and sparkling words from another without ever acquiring a coherent system of thought. In fact, on closer inspection clear patterns of thought and lines of affinity between most of his major sources emerge. Many of Traherne's sources are exactly what one might expect from a well-educated man of his day – Plato and Aristotle, Augustine and Aquinas, the Bible, that blend of classical and religious that marked a traditional seventeenth-century education. There are also the works cited in the *Centuries* in Traherne's account of his studies at university: Albert Magnus, Galileo, Hevelius, Galen, Hippocrates, Orpheus, Homer, Lilly. To this list we may now add the scientific discoveries of the likes of Boyle and Harvey, Willis and White mentioned in *The Kingdom of God* as well as those theologians, Twisse, Sanderson, Hoard and Hammond, whose interest in the Calvinist/Arminian debate Traherne traces in *A Sober View of Dr Twisse*. That Hooker, Herbert and Andrewes also appear in the new Lambeth manuscript lends further credence to the notion that far from being remote from his times, Traherne engaged intimately with the works of his fellow theologians and poets and that his own work was bred in the bed of theirs.

In the late 1660s, just before he became chaplain to Bridgeman, Traherne translated notes from the Renaissance philosopher Ficino's commentaries on Plato and the opening part of the *Argumentum* to his translation of Hermes Trismegistus into a small notebook. The *Ficino Notebook*, as it is now known, is just one example of Traherne's connections with the Italian Renaissance tradition. This line of thought originates in the collection of ancient hermetical writings attributed to Hermes Trismegistus (or Hermes thrice great), whose subjects range from alchemy to natural philosophy and spirituality. From this mixed bag the fifteenth-century Italian Ficino and his follower Pico della Mirandola drew a keen sense of the great capacity of the human soul and the high position of humankind in the universe, and developed the great Renaissance ideal of the human person that was to shape much of Western thought for centuries to come. That Traherne studied Ficino and Hermes is clear from the existence of the *Ficino Notebook*; in Traherne's *Commonplace Book* too there are many references to Hermes Trismegistus, sometimes indicated simply by a 'Tris' scribbled hastily in the margin. And Pico appears most pointedly in those lofty passages in the *Centuries* in which the human is described as having the power 'to hav what he desires and to be what he Wisheth'.

But what is most interesting is that these writings of Hermes, of Ficino and Pico fed directly into the thinking of that group of seventeenth-century Cambridge theologians known as the Cambridge Platonists, and the later Latitudinarians. Traherne's affinity with the Cambridge Platonists has often been noted.[5] Influenced, as Traherne also was, by Plato and Plotinus, who married Platonic philosophy with Christianity, the Cambridge Platonists understood their Christian faith as the fruition of a revelation that began in pre-Christian teachings of the most ancient wisdom and continued through the Enlightenment. All that was good in pre-Christian teaching they tried to take on board, just as they also embraced the new discoveries of their own day. This openness, their emphasis on the importance of free will and their trust in human reason made their theology particularly suited to an age of intellectual exploration. It offered a means of bringing together the new knowledge and the old faith that appealed to Traherne. He directly cites several of the Cambridge Platonists and of the later Latitudinarians Henry

More, Thomas Jackson and Edward Stillingfleet along with Theophilus Gale in his works and notebooks.[6] From this chain of texts all the way back to Hermes, and from this company of thinkers Traherne gleaned his sense of humankind as the pinnacle of creation, that golden link between the spiritual and physical worlds. At about the same time that Traherne was studying Hermes and Ficino – incidentally texts also studied by the Cambridge Platonist Henry More – he was appointed to Bridgeman's household. It may be partly this affinity to Cambridge Platonism and its subsequent Latitudinarianism that fitted Traherne for his appointment to Bridgeman's household since Traherne's predecessor, Hezekiah Burton, was a minor Latitudinarian.

To say that Traherne shared much with the Cambridge Platonists is not to suggest that he is a pure Platonist; in fact much of his writing on happiness derives directly from the opposite camp – Aristotle and Aquinas. Inspired by the infinite, the one and the good, he is also passionate about the material and the finite, constantly aware of the immanence of God in creation and convinced of the possibility of heaven here in the diverse beauties of the material world. Here as elsewhere, repeatedly and ultimately, Traherne resorts to paradox. And his paradoxes place him in the fellowship of Nicholas of Cusa and of Meister Eckhart, of Henry Suso and of Julian of Norwich, mystics whose minds also hold the contradictories of both/and in splendid tension.

To this growing list of Traherne's sources we must add the Church Fathers. Augustine perceived that there was in every soul a weight drawing it constantly until it found its natural place of rest. 'My weight is my love,' he wrote. 'By it I am carried wherever I am carried'; and in this confession one hears intimations of the 'som Great Thing' that calls Traherne's soul too. The whole notion of delight and desire that percolates in Traherne is drawing on this tradition. But there are others: the insatiable reach towards infinity that we see in Traherne is reminiscent of the soul's stretching forth that is so characteristic of Gregory of Nyssa. Gregory of Nanzianzus (329–89) Traherne cites too, as well as Irenaeus. Traherne used Irenaeus' model for discerning heresies in his polemical work *Roman Forgeries*. But there is much more that the two men have in common: most importantly, it is to Irenaeus that Traherne is indebted for his notion of the fall and of redemption. For both Traherne and Irenaeus the great catastrophe is not the fall of Adam but the subsequent inevitable falls of each person as they repeatedly sin against God; for both men sin is basically a misevaluation of things; the atonement is not so much about Christ defeating the old Adam as it is about Christ assimilating himself to humankind and humankind to himself; and redemption is innocence restored. These views mark a departure from the traditional view of human sinfulness as set out by Augustine and his followers. Where Augustine sees humankind as conceived in sin and corrupt from birth Traherne, writing out of, as he puts it, 'that Divine Light wherewith I was born', affirms an essentially good creation.

Traherne's voluminous notes on Bacon in the *Early Notebook* reveal an interest in Bacon's views on everything from science to celibacy. The Spanish Jesuit Puente is a source for Traherne's *Thanksgivings* and the *Church's Year-Book*; and there are striking similarities between *Inducements to Retiredness* and the devotional writings of Thomas à Kempis whom Traherne cites in the first *Century*. But one of the most significant sources of inspiration for Traherne is a source that has also inspired thousands of his readers, the Psalms. The poetic resolves in *Inducements to Retiredness* and in *The Kingdom of God* are modelled directly on the Psalms and sections of his *Centuries* make clear his spiritual affinity with David. Above all Traherne wanted to be a man after God's own heart: 'Oh that I might be a David,' he cries with august and infinite desire.

What strikes me again and again as I consider Traherne's vast array of sources and influences is his voracious appetite for learning and a conviction that every discovery could lead one further into truth. There is in him no fear of knowledge, of science or of exploration. He has a tremendous ability to embrace new scientific discoveries and to combine this with his interest in everything from the *Hermetica* to classical Scholastic scholarship – those things he learned 'in the Scholes'. All point to a person of unshakeable faith and intellectual honesty. But varied and interesting as these academic and theological sources are, we should never forget the immediate influences that shaped his work. The events of his day, from the huge and national such as the Restoration of the king to the ordinary and personal: 'I have seen in plays and vain Romances . . .' inform all of his work. And it is to these events we now turn.

Historical Context

We of the late twentieth and early twenty-first centuries have witnessed an increasing privatization of faith and secularization of politics. Spirituality has become, for many, a deeply personal journey into self and towards some supreme other. Meanwhile politics is increasingly conceived as divorced from any religion. It is about the secular good of society which can exist separately from the spiritual welfare of the people. But Traherne wrote in an age of political turmoil and religious strife when every belief wore political dress, when priests could be spies and congregations armies. Writers and poets then are men of their age; turbulent in an age of turbulence, open in an age of exploration, but always informed by the conflicts around them; and there is a passion in their poetry that I believe has something to do with this fact. Perhaps because belief was something you might die for it was also more passionately something you might live for. This may especially be true of Traherne who lived through the Civil War (1642–49). Traherne was about 6 when it started and 13 when it finished – all his boyhood days would have been coloured by the battles and the bloodshed of war.

When the Puritans defeated both Church and Charles I, abolished the one and beheaded the other, religious and political choices merged further. Traherne's friend Susanna Hopton, who was a secret agent for the defeated Royalists, showed her aversion to the Puritan victory by converting to Catholicism. Upon the Restoration, she converted back to the Church of England. She was not alone. Many people changed their politics and their religion as the wind blew; others changed for life. In his early adult life Traherne was educated at Brasenose under a strictly Puritan head and must have been considered suitably Puritan to be presented to the living of Credenhill by the Commissioners for the Approbation of Public Preachers, supported by a sufficient number of eminent Puritan preachers. And yet, he seems gradually to have changed his position between his presentation to Credenhill in 1657 and 1660. Five of the six ministers who provided certificates for him were so staunchly Puritan as to be ejected from their livings after the Restoration in 1660; whereas Traherne seemed eager for episcopal ordination. He was ordained in October 1660, well in advance of being obliged to do so, and conformed to the Act of Uniformity made in August 1662.

I do not think this is merely about Traherne protecting his own career. For there is real joy in Traherne's exclamations at the thought of the return of the king. Perhaps he had imbibed the spirit of his birthplace; after all, during the war Hereford had been a bastion of mostly ineffectual but heartfelt Royalist support. Certainly Traherne's writings simmer with a love of kingship; the kingdom and king are images to which he continually returns. The symbols of power, the throne, crowns and sceptres are part of this, but there is a love too of the pleasure and pageantry of kings, the feasts and treasures, which are signs of the wealth and prosperity of the kingdom, the king's people, their towns and trades. For Traherne the health and wealth of the king is not in opposition to the well-being of the people. In Traherne's passionate support of a national church his desire for political stability and civic order is married to his sacred convictions.

The Select Meditations show a clear preoccupation with the politics of his turbulent times. And his interest in then current theological debates is evident in *A Sober View*. *The Kingdom of God* abounds in references to new scientific and philosophical discoveries which he never saw as a threat to faith. In one way the hitherto 'unconnected' Traherne has never been more a writer of his own day. And yet he is also strangely a writer of our time. It is not just that he was discovered again at the turn of the twentieth century after centuries of near oblivion, and that the discovery of his work continues, although that does give a modern reader the feeling that he is somehow new. There is something in what he says that rings bells with a twenty-first-century mind. In the terrorism of our own age we can taste the terrible power bred in the marriage of religious belief and political struggle. There is also something modern in Traherne's thought. Much of his poetry seems to have anticipated later periods of literary history. The poetic possibilities of his theme of early innocence, for example, not fully explored until more than a century later when Blake and Wordsworth, who could not have known Traherne's poetry, re-echoed so much of his thought. And ideas which were for him bold sallies into the future have become commonplace to us now. Statements such as 'it is not our Parents Loyns, so much as our Parents lives that Enthrals and Blinds us' presage the insights of modern psychology and surprise us by their completely contemporary sentiment. But more importantly, he writes with a vitality and entire sincerity that appeal to a modern reader's need for integrity. He writes to a Christian audience, and a shared faith will certainly make his writings resonate more deeply for some readers. But the quest for happiness and its concomitant motions of desire are universal. There is in Traherne a call towards the infinite, towards simplicity and present happiness that reverberates across human experience so that persons of all faiths and of none may derive benefit from his work.

This anthology begins with the most familiar and best loved of Traherne's works and moves gradually towards the newest discoveries, roughly following the order in which Traherne became known to the twentieth century. This arrangement of texts reflects something of the gradual shift that is occurring from studying him primarily as a poet to studying him again as a theologian. I hope that organizing the material by work rather than by theme will make it easier for the reader to find the things they are looking for as well as give a sense of the different kinds of styles and voices Traherne used in his various works.

Notes

1. See Malcolm Day (1982), *Thomas Traherne* (Boston: Twayne Publishers), p. 1 and Gladys Wade (1944), *Thomas Traherne* (Princeton: Princeton University Press), pp. 32–37.

2. I am indebted to Dr Julia Smith for these insights into Traherne's biography.
3. See Julia Smith's note (1997) in the introduction to *Select Meditations* (Manchester: Carcanet), pp. xii–xiii and the exclamations in meditation II.38, 'O my T.G. O my S.H. O my brother!'
4. Leigh DeNeef (1988), *Traherne in Dialogue: Heidegger, Lacan, and Derrida* (Durham and London: Duke University Press), pp. 5, 6.
5. See Carol Marks (1966), 'Thomas Traherne and Cambridge Platonism', *Publications of the Modern Language Association of America* 81, pp. 521–34 and T. O. Beachcroft (1930), 'Traherne and the Cambridge Platonists', *Dublin Review* 186, pp. 278–90, among others.
6. More, Jackson and Gale are quoted in Traherne's *Commonplace Book*, Gale again in the *Commentaries of Heaven*, Stillingfleet at the front of *Roman Forgeries*. Parts of *The Kingdom of God* rely heavily on Gale.

Selections from the *Centuries of Meditations*

In the *Centuries* all of Traherne's main themes – innocence, infinity, felicity, desire, enjoyment of the world, love – appear. And right from the start they are interconnected. At the opening of the first *Century* early innocence is described as capacity, a kind of hopeful emptiness that foreshadows his final meditations on infinity in the unfinished fifth *Century*. The 'som Great Thing' that pulls him and his reader along suggests not only the fruit of the quest for happiness, but also its motion of desire. The second *Century* with its meditations on love depicts the soul extending towards God and God towards the soul. In the third *Century*, often called 'autobiographical', his love of creation and his quest for felicity intermingle. Though Traherne shifts voices in the fourth *Century*, referring to himself as 'he', his themes are just the same, here worked out in action since his concern in the fourth *Century* is not the finding but the practice of godly principles.

The First Century

1

An Empty Book is like an Infants Soul, in which any Thing may be Written. It is Capable of all Things, but containeth Nothing. I hav a Mind to fill this with Profitable Wonders. And since Love made you put it into my Hands I will fill it with those Truths you Love, without Knowing them: and with those Things which, if it be Possible, shall shew my Lov; To you, in Communicating most *Enriching Truths*; to Truth, in Exalting Her Beauties in such a Soul.

2

Do not Wonder, that I promise to fill it, with those Truths you love,
but know not: For tho it be a Maxime in the Scholes, That there is
no Lov of a thing unknown; yet I hav found, that Things unknown
have a Secret Influence on the Soul: and like the Centre of the
5 Earth unseen, violently Attract it. We lov we know not what: and
therfore evry Thing allures us. As Iron at a Distance is drawn by the
Loadstone, there being some Invisible Communications between
them: So is there in us a World of Lov to somwhat, tho we know
not what in the World that should be. There are Invisible Ways of
10 Conveyance, by which som Great Thing doth touch our Souls, and
by which we tend to it. Do you not feel your self Drawn with the
Expectation and Desire of som Great Thing?

21

By the very Right of your Sences you Enjoy the World. Is not the
Beauty of the Hemisphere present to your Ey? Doth not the Glory
of the Sun pay Tribut to your Sight. Is not the Vision of the
WORLD an Amiable Thing? Do not the Stars shed Influences to
5 Perfect the Air? Is not that a marvellous Body to Breath in? To visit
the Lungs: repair the Spirits: revive the Sences: Cool the Blood: fill
the Empty Spaces between the Earth and Heavens; and yet giv
Liberty to all Objects? Prize these first: and you shall Enjoy the
Residue. Glory, Dominion, Power, Wisdom, Honor, Angels, Souls,
10 Kingdoms, Ages. *Be faithfull in a little, and you shall be Master over
much.* If you be not faithfull in esteeming these, who shall put into
your Hands the true Treasures. If you be Negligent in Prizing these,
you will be Negligent in Prizing all. There is a Diseas in Him who
Despiseth present mercies, which till it be cured, he can never be
15 Happy. He esteemeth nothing that he hath, but is ever Gaping after
more: which when he hath He despiseth in like manner.
Insatiableness is Good, but not Ingratitud.

22

It is of the Nobility of Mans Soul that He is Insatiable · for he hath a
Benefactor so Prone to Give, that He delighteth in us for Asking.
Do not your Inclinations tell you that the WORLD is yours? Do

Scholes, in the Scholastic tradition

you not covet all? Do you not long to hav it; to Enjoy it; to
Overcom it? To what End do Men gather Riches, but to Multiplie
more? Do they not like Pyrrhus the King of Epire, adde hous to
hous and Lands to Lands, that they may get it all? It is storied of
that Prince, that having conceived a Purpose to invade Italy, he sent
for Cineas, a Philosopher and the Kings friend: to whom he
communicated his Designe, and desired his Counsel. Cineas asked
him to what Purpose he invaded Italie? He said, To Conquer it.
And what will you do when you hav Conquerd it? Go into France
said the King, and Conquer that. And what will you do when you
have Conquerd France? Conquer Germany. And what then? said
the Philosopher. Conquer Spain. I perceive said Cineas, you mean
to conquer all the World. What will you do when you have
conquerd all? Why then said the King we will return, and Enjoy
our selvs at Quiet in our own Land. So you may now said the
Philosopher without all this adoe. Yet could he not Divert him till
he was ruind by the Romans. Thus men get one Hundred Pound
a year that they may get another; and having two covet Eight, and
there is no End of all their Labor; becaus the Desire of their Soul
is Insatiable. Like Alexander the Great they must hav all: and when
they hav got it all be quiet. And may they not do all this before they
begin? Nay it would be well, if they could be Quiet. But if after all,
they shall be like the stars, that are seated on high, but hav no Rest,
what gain they more, but Labor for their Trouble? It was wittily
fained that that Yong man sate down and Cried for more Worlds.
So insatiable is Man that Millions will not Pleas him. They are no
more then so many Tennis-Balls, in Comparison of the Greatness
and Highness of his Soul.

27

You never Enjoy the World aright, till you see how a Sand
Exhibiteth the Wisdom and Power of God: And Prize in evry
Thing the Service which they do you, by Manifesting His Glory
and Goodness to your Soul, far more then the Visible Beauty on
their Surface, or the Material Services, they can do your Body.
Wine by its Moysture quencheth my Thirst, whether I consider it
or no: but to see it flowing from his Lov who gav it unto Man,

Quencheth the Thirst even of the Holy Angels. To consider it, is
to Drink it Spiritualy. To Rejoice in its Diffusion is to be of a
10 Publick Mind. And to take Pleasure in all the Benefits it doth to
all is Heavenly · for so they do in Heaven. To do so, is to be Divine
and Good · and to imitat our Infinit and Eternal Father.

28

Your Enjoyment of the World is never right, till evry Morning
you awake in Heaven: see your self in your fathers Palace: and
look upon the Skies and the Earth and the Air, as Celestial Joys:
having such a Reverend Esteem of all, as if you were among the
5 Angels. The Bride of a Monarch, in her Husbands Chamber, hath
no such Causes of Delight as you.

29

You never Enjoy the World aright, till the Sea it self floweth in
your Veins, till you are Clothed with the Heavens, and Crowned
with the Stars: and perceiv your self to be the Sole Heir of the
whole World: and more then so, becaus Men are in it who are
5 evry one Sole Heirs, as well as you. Till you can Sing and Rejoyce
and Delight in GOD, as Misers do in Gold, and Kings in Scepters,
you never Enjoy the World.

30

Till your Spirit filleth the whole World, and the Stars are your
Jewels, till you are as Familiar with the Ways of God in all Ages as
with your Walk and Table: till you are intimatly Acquainted with
that Shady Nothing out of which the World was made: till you lov
5 Men so as to Desire their Happiness, with a Thirst equal to the
zeal of your own: till you Delight in GOD for being Good to all:
you never Enjoy the World. Till you more feel it then your Privat
Estate, and are more present in the Hemisphere, Considering the
Glories and the Beauties there, then in your own Hous. Till you
10 remember how lately you were made, and how wonderfull it was
when you came into it: and more rejoyce in the Palace of your
Glory, then if it had been made but to Day Morning.

31

Yet further, you never Enjoy the World aright, till you so lov the Beauty of Enjoying it, that you are Covetous and Earnest to Persuade others to Enjoy it. And so perfectly hate the Abominable Corruption of Men in Despising it, that you had rather suffer the flames of Hell then willingly be Guilty of their Error. There is so much Blindness, and Ingratitud, and Damned folly in it. The World is a Mirror of infinit Beauty, yet no Man sees it. It is a Temple of Majesty yet no Man regards it. It is a Region of Light and Peace, did not Men Disquiet it. It is the Paradice of God. It is more to Man since he is faln, then it was before. It is the Place of Angels, and the Gate of Heaven. When Jacob waked out of His Dream, he said, *God is here and I wist it not. How Dreadfull is this Place! This is none other, then the Hous of God, and the Gate of Heaven.*

40

Socrates was wont to say, *They are most Happy and neerest the Gods that needed Nothing.* And coming once up into the Exchange at Athens, where they that Traded Asked Him, What will you Buy; what do you lack? After he had Gravely Walkt up into the Middle, spreading forth his Hands and turning about, *Good Gods*, saith he, *who would hav thought there were so many Things in the World which I do not want!* And so left the Place under the Reproach of Nature. He was wont to say, *That Happiness consisted not in Having Many, but in Needing the Fewest Things: for the Gods Needed Nothing at all, and they were most like them that least Needed.* We Needed Heaven and Earth, our Sences, Such Souls and Such Bodies, with infinit Riches in the Image of God to be Enjoyed: Which God of his Mercy having freely prepared, they are most Happy that so live in the Enjoyment of those, as to need no Accidental Trivial Thing. No Splendors, Pomps and Vanities. Socrates perhaps being an Heathen, knew not that all Things proceeded from God to Man, and by Man returned to God: but we that know it: must need All Things as God doth that we may receiv them with Joy, and liv in His Image.

His Dream, Genesis 28.12

41

As Pictures are made Curious by Lights and Shades, which without
Shades, could not be: so is Felicitie composed of Wants and
Supplies, without which Mixture there could be no Felicity. Were
there no Needs, Wants would be Wanting themselvs: And Supplies
Superfluous. Want being the Parent of Celestial Treasure. It is very
Strange; Want it self is a Treasure in Heaven: And so Great an one,
that without it there could be no Treasure. GOD did infinitly for
us, when He made us to Want like GODS, that like GODS, we
might be satisfied. The Heathen DIETIES wanted nothing, and
were therfore unhappy; For they had no Being. But the LORD
GOD of Israel the Living and True GOD, was from all Eternity, and
from all Eternity Wanted like a GOD. He Wanted the
Communication of His Divine Essence, and Persons to Enjoy it.
He Wanted Worlds, He wanted Spectators, He wanted Joys, He
wanted Treasures. He wanted, yet he wanted not, for he had them.

42

This is very strange that GOD should Want · for in Him is the
Fulness of all Blessedness. He overfloweth Eternaly. His Wants are
as Glorious as Infinit. Perfectiv needs that are in His Nature, and
ever Blessed, becaus always Satisfied. He is from Eternity full of
Want: Or els He would not be full of Treasure. Infinit Want is the
very Ground and Caus of infinit Treasure. It is Incridible, yet very
Plain: Want is the Fountain of all His Fulness. Want in GOD is a
Treasure to us. For had there been no Need He would not hav
Created the World, nor Made us, nor Manifested his Wisdom, nor
Exercised his Power, nor Beautified Eternity, nor prepared the Joys
of Heaven. But He Wanted Angels and Men, Images, Companions.
And these He had from all Eternitie.

43

Infinit Wants Satisfied Produce infinit Joys; And, in the Possession of
those Joys, are infinit Joys themselvs. *The Desire Satisfied is a Tree of
Life.* Desire imports som thing absent: and a Need of what is Absent.
GOD was never without this Tree of Life. He did Desire infinitly ·
yet He was never without the Fruits of this Tree, which are the Joys

it produced. I must lead you out of this, into another World, to learn your Wants. For till you find them you will never be Happy. Wants themselvs being sacred Occasions and Means of Felicitie.

44

You must Want like a GOD, that you may be Satisfied like GOD. Were you not made in His *Image*? He is infinitly Glorious, becaus all His Wants and Supplies are at the same time in his Nature from Eternity. He had, and from Eternity He was without all His Treasures. From Eternity He needed them, and from Eternity He ₅ enjoyed them. For all Eternity is at once in Him · both the Empty Durations before the World was made, and the full ones after. His Wants are as Lively as His Enjoyments: And always present with Him. For His Life is Perfect, and He feels them both. His Wants put a Lustre upon His Enjoyments, and make them infinit. His ₁₀ Enjoyments being infinit Crown his Wants, and make them Beautifull even to GOD Himself. His Wants and Enjoyments being always present, are Delightfull to each other, stable Immutable Perfectiv of each other, and Delightfull to Him. Who being Eternal and Immutable, Enjoyeth all His Wants and Treasures ₁₅ together. His Wants never Afflict Him, His Treasures never Disturb Him. His Wants always Delight Him, His Treasures never Cloy Him. The Sence of His Wants is always as Great, as if his Treasures were removed: and as lively upon Him. The Sence of His Wants, as it Enlargeth His Life, so it infuseth a Valu, and continual Sweetness ₂₀ into the Treasures He Enjoyeth.

45

This is a Lesson long enough: which you may be all your Life in Learning, and to all Eternity in Practising. *Be Sensible of your Wants, that you may be sensible of your Treasures.* He is most like GOD that is sensible of evry Thing. Did you not from all Eternity Want som one to give you a Being? Did you not Want one to give you a ₅ Glorious Being? Did you not from all Eternity Want som one to giv you infinit Treasures? And som one to give you Spectators,

be sensible of, be cognizant of, perceive, be fully aware of

Companions, Enjoyers? Did you not Want a Dietie, to make them
Sweet and Honorable by His infinit Wisdom? What you wanted
10 from all Eternity, be sensible of to all Eternity. Let your Wants be
present from Everlasting. Is not this a Strange Life to which I call
you? Wherin you are to be present with Things that were before
the World was made? And at once present even like GOD with
infinit Wants and infinit Treasures? Be present with your Want of
15 a Diety, and you shall be present with the Dietie. You shall Adore
and Admire Him, Enjoy and Prize Him; Believ in Him, and
Delight in Him: See Him to be the Fountain of all your Joys · and
the Head of all your Treasures.

46

It was His Wisdom made you Need the Sun. It was His Goodness
made you need the Sea. Be Sensible of what you need, or Enjoy
neither. Consider how much you need them. For thence they
Derive their Value. Suppose the Sun were Extinguished: or the Sea
5 were Drie. There would be no Light, no Beauty, no Warmth, no
Fruits, no Flowers, no Pleasant Gardens, Feasts, or Prospects. No
Wine no Oyl no Bread, no Life, no Motion. Would you not give
all the Gold and Silver in the Indies for such a Treasure? Prize it
now you have it, at that Rate, and you shall be a Grateful
10 Creature: Nay you shall be a Divine and Heavenly Person. For
they in Heaven do Prize Blessings when they hav them. They in
Earth when they hav them Prize them not, They in Hell Prize
them, when they hav them not.

47

To hav Blessings and to Prize them is to be in Heaven; To hav
them, and not to prize them, is to be in Hell, I would say upon
Earth: To prize them and not to hav them, is to be in Hell. Which
is Evident by the Effects. To Prize Blessings while we hav them is
5 to Enjoy them, and the effect therof is Contentation Pleasure
Thanksgiving Happiness. To Prize them when they are gone
produceth Envy, Covetousness, Repining, Ingratitud, Vexation,
Miserie. But it was no Great Mistake to say, That to hav Blessings,
and not to Prize them is to be in Hell. For it maketh them

ineffectual, as if they were Absent. Yea in som respect it is Worse 10
then to be in Hell. It is more vicious, and more Irrational.

55

The Contemplation of Eternity maketh the Soul Immortal. Whose
Glory it is, that it can see before and after its Existence into Endless
Spaces. Its Sight is its Presence. And therfore is the Presence of the
Understanding Endless, becaus its Sight is so. O what Glorious
Creatures should we be, could we be present in Spirit with all 5
Eternity! How Wise, would we esteem this presence of the
understanding, to be more real then that of our Bodies! When my
Soul is in Eden with our first Parents, I my self am there in a Blessed
Maner. When I walk with Enoch, and see his Translation, I am
Transported with Him. The present Age is too little to contain it. I 10
can visit Noah in His Ark, and swim upon the Waters of the
Deluge. I can see Moses with his Rod, and the children of Israel
passing thorow the Sea. I can Enter into Aarons Tabernacle, and
Admire the Mysteries of the Holy Place. I can Travail over the Land
of Canaan, and see it overflowing with Milk and Hony; I can visit 15
Solomon in his Glory, and go into his Temple, and view the sitting
of His servants, and Admire the Magnificence and Glory of his
Kingdom. No Creature but one like unto the Holy Angels can see
into all Ages. Sure this Power was not given in vain · but for some
Wonderfull Purpose; worthy of itself to Enjoy and fathom. Would 20
Men consider what GOD hath don, they would be Ravished in
Spirit with the Glory of His Doings. For Heaven and Earth are full
of the Majesty of His Glory. And how Happy would Men be could
they see and Enjoy it! But abov all these our Saviors Cross is the
Throne of Delights. That Centre of Eternity, *That Tree of Life* in the 25
midst of the Paradice of GOD!

56

There are we Entertained with the Wonder of all Ages. There we
enter into the Heart of the Univers. There we Behold the
Admiration of Angels. There we find the Price and Elixar of our
Joys. As on evry side of the Earth all Heavy things tend to the
Centre; so all Nations ought on evry Side to flow in unto it. It is not 5

by going with the feet, but by Journeys of the Soul, that we Travail
thither. By withdrawing our Thoughts from Wandering in the
Streets of this World, to the Contemplation and Serious Meditation
of his Bloody Sufferings. Where the Carcase is thither will the
Eagles be Gathered together. Our Eys must be towards it, our Hearts
set upon it, our Affections Drawn and our Thoughts and Minds
united to it. When I am lifted up saith the Son of man I will draw
all Men unto me. As fishes are Drawn out of the Water, as Jeremie
was Drawn out of the Dungeon, as S. Peters Sheet was Drawn up
into heaven; so shall we be Drawn by that Sight from Ignorance and
Sin and Earthly vanities, idle Sports Companions Feasts and
Pleasures, to the Joyfull Contemplation of that Eternal Object. But
by what Cords? The Cords of a Man, and the Cords of Lov.

57

As Eagles are Drawn by the Sent of a Carcais, As Children are
Drawn together by the Sight of a Lion, As People flock to a
Coronation, and as a Man is Drawn to his Beloved Object, so
ought we. As the Sick are Drawn by the Credit of a Physician, as
the Poor are Drawn by the Liberality of a King, as the Devout are
Drawn by the fame of the Holy, and as the Curious are Drawn by
the Nois of a Miracle so ought we. As the stones were Drawn to
the Building of Thebes by the Melodie of Amphion, as the
Hungry are Drawn with the Desire of a Feast, and the Pitifull
Drawn to a Wofull Spectacle so ought we. What Visible Chains or
Cords draw these? What Invisible Links allure? They follow all, or
flock together of their own accord. And shall not we much more?
Who would not be Drawn to the Gate of Heaven, were it open
to receiv him? Yet nothing compels Him, but that which forceth
the Angels · Commoditie and Desire. For these are Things which
the Angels desire to look into. And of Men it is Written, They shall
look on Him whom they hav Peirced. Verily the Israelites did not
more Clearly see the Brazen Serpent upon the Pole in the
Wilderness, then we may our Savior upon the Cross. The Serpent

S. Peters Sheet, Acts 11.11

was seen with their Eys, the Slayer of the Serpent is seen with our   20
Souls. They had less need to see the one, then we to see the other.

58
The Cross is the Abyss of Wonders, the Centre of Desires, the
Schole of Virtues, the Hous of Wisdom, the Throne of Lov, the
Theatre of Joys and the Place of Sorrows; It is the Root of
Happiness, and the Gate of Heaven.

59
Of all the Things in Heaven and Earth it is the most Peculiar. It is
the most Exalted of all Objects. It is an Ensign lifted up for all
Nations, to it shall the Gentiles seek, His Rest shall be Glorious:
the Dispersed of Judah shall be gathered together to it, from the
four Corners of the Earth. If Lov be the Weight of the Soul, and   5
its Object the Centre · All Eys and Hearts may convert and turn
unto this Object: cleave unto this Centre, and by it enter into
Rest. There we might see all Nations Assembled with their Eys
and Hearts upon it. There we may see Gods Goodness Wisdom
and Power: yea his Mercy and Anger displayed. There we may see   10
Mans Sin and infinit value. His Hope and Fear, his Misery and
Happiness. There we might see the Rock of Ages, and the Joys of
Heaven. There we may see a Man Loving all the World, and a
GOD Dying for Mankind(.) There we may see all Types and
Ceremonies, figures and Prophesies. And all Kingdoms Adoring a   15
Malefactor: An Innocent Malefactor, yet the Greatest in the
World. There we may see the most Distant Things in Eternity
united: all Mysteries at once couched together and Explained. The
only reason why this Glorious Object is so Publickly Admired by
Churches and Kingdoms, and so little thought of by Particular   20
men, is becaus it is truly the most Glorious. It is the Root of
Comforts, and the Fountain of Joys. It is the only Supreme and
Soveraign Spectacle in all Worlds. It is a Well of Life beneath in
which we may see the face of Heaven abov: and the only Mirror,
wherin all things appear in their Proper Colors · that is sprinkled   25
in the Blood of our Lord and Savior.

60

The Cross of Christ is the Jacobs ladder by which we Ascend into the Highest Heavens. There we see Joyfull Patriarchs, Expecting Saints, and Prophets Ministering, Apostles Publishing and Doctors Teaching. All Nations concentering, and Angels Praising. That
5 Cross is a Tree set on fire with invisible flame, that Illuminateth all the World. The Flame is Lov. The Lov in His Bosom who died on it. In the light of which we see how to possess all the Things in Heaven and Earth after His Similitud. For He that Suffered on it, was the Son of GOD as you are: tho He seemed a Mortal Man.
10 He had Acquaintance and Relations as you hav, but He was a Lover of Men and Angels. Was He not the Son of GOD and Heir of the Whole World? To this poor Bleeding Naked Man did all the Corn and Wine and Oyl, and Gold and Silver in the World minister in an Invisible Maner, even as he was exposed Lying and
15 Dying upon the Cross.

61

Here you learn all Patience, Meekness, Self Denial, Courage, Prudence, Zeal, Lov, Charity, Contempt of the World, Joy, Penitence, Contrition, Modestie, Fidelity, Constancy Perseverance, Holiness, Contentation and Thanksgiving. With whatsoever els is
5 requisit for a Man, a Christian or a King. This Man Bleeding here was Tutor to King Charles the Martyr: and Great Master to S. Paul the Convert who learned of Him Activity, and Zeal unto all Nations. Well therfore may we take up with this Prospect, and from hence behold all the Things in Heaven and Earth. Here we learn
10 to imitat Jesus in his Lov unto all.

The Second Century

62

Lov is the true Means by which the World is Enjoyed. Our Lov to others, and Others Lov to us. We ought therfore abov all Things to get acquainted with the Nature of Lov · for Lov is the Root and Foundation of Nature: Lov is the Soul of Life, and Crown of

Rewards. If we cannot be satisfied in the Nature of Lov we can
never be satisfied at all. The very End for which GOD made the
World was that He might Manifest His Lov. Unless therfore we
can be satisfied with his Lov so manifested we can never be
satisfied. There are many Glorious Excellencies in the Material
World, but without Lov they are all Abortiv. We might spend Ages
in Contemplating the Nature of the Sun, and entertain our selvs
many yeers with the Beauty of the Stars, and Services of the Sea:
but the Soul of Man is above all these, it comprehendeth all Ages
in a Moment; and unless it perceiv somthing more Excellent, is
very Desolat. All Worlds being but a Silent Wilderness, without
som living Thing, more Sweet and Blessed after which it Aspireth.
Lov in the fountain, and Lov in the End is the Glory of the World,
and the Soul of Joy. Which it infinitly preferreth abov all Worlds,
and delighteth in, and loveth to Contemplat, more then all Visible
Beings that are Possible. So that you must be sure to see Causes,
wherfore infinitly to be Delighted with the Lov of GOD, if ever
you would be Happy.

63

See Causes also wherfore to be Delighted in your Lov to Men,
and Lov of Men to you. For the World serves you to this End, that
you might lov them and be Beloved of them. And unless you are
pleased with the End for which the World serves you, you can
never be pleased with the Means leading to that End. Abov all
things therfore Contemplat the Glory of Loving Men, and of
being Beloved of them. For this End our Savior Died, and for this
End He came into the World, that you might be restored from
Hatred, which is the Greatest Misery. From the Hatred of GOD
and Men which was due for Sin, and from the Misery of Hating
GOD and Men; for to Hate and be Hated is the Greatest Misery.
The Necessity of Hating GOD and Men being the Greatest
Bondage, that Hell can impose.

64

When you lov men, the World Quickly becometh yours: and your
self becom a Greater Treasure then the World is. For all their

Persons are your Treasures, and all the Things in Heaven and Earth that serv them, are yours. For those are the Riches of Lov, which
5   minister to its Object.

65

You are as Prone to lov, as the Sun is to shine. It being the most Delightfull and Natural Employment of the Soul of Man: without which you are Dark and Miserable, Consider therfore the Extent of Lov, its Vigor and Excellency. For certainly He that Delights not
5   in Lov makes vain the Univers, and is of Necessity to Himself the Greatest Burden. The Whole World ministers to you as the Theatre of your Lov. It sustains you and all Objects that you may continu to lov them. Without which it were Better for you to hav no Being. Life without Objects is Sensible Emptiness. Objects
10   without Lov are the Delusion of Life. The Objects of Lov are its Greatest Treasures: and without Lov it is impossible they should be Treasures. For the Objects which we lov are the Pleasing Objects, and Delightfull Things. And whatsoever is not pleasing and delightfull to us can be no Treasure. Nay it is Distastefull, and
15   Worse then Nothing, since we had rather it should hav no Being.

66

That Violence wherwith som times a man doteth upon one Creature, is but a little spark of that lov, even towards all, which lurketh in His Nature. We are made to lov: both to satisfy the Necessity of our Activ Nature, and to answer the Beauties in evry
5   Creature. By Lov our souls are married and sodderd to the creatures: and it is our Duty like GOD to be united to them all. We must lov them infinitly but in God, and for God: and God in them: namely all His Excellencies Manifested in them. When we dote upon the Perfections and Beauties of som one Creature: we
10   do not lov that too much, but other things too little. Never was any thing in this World loved too much, but many Things hav been loved in a fals Way: and all in too short a Measure.

Sensible, of the senses

67

Suppose a River or a Drop of Water, an Apple or a Sand, an Ear
of Corn, or an Herb: GOD knoweth infinit Excellencies in it
more then we: He seeth how it relateth to Angels and Men; How
it proceedeth from the most perfect Lover to the most Perfectly
Beloved; how it representeth all His Attributs; How it conduceth   5
in its place, by the best of Means to the Best of Ends: And for this
Caus it cannot be Beloved too much. GOD the Author and GOD
the End is to be Beloved in it: Angels and Men are to be Beloved
in it: And it is highly to be Esteemed for all their Sakes. O what a
Treasure is evry Sand when truly understood! Who can lov any   10
Thing that God made too much? His infinit Goodness and
Wisdom and Power and Glory are in it. What a World would this
be, were evry thing Beloved as it ought to be!

68

Suppose a Curious and fair Woman. Som have seen the Beauties
of Heaven, in such a Person. It is a vain Thing to say they loved
too much. I dare say there are 10000 Beauties in that Creature
which they hav not seen. They loved it not too much but upon
fals causes. Nor so much upon fals ones, as only upon som little   5
ones. They lov a Creature for Sparkling Eys and Curled Hair,
Lillie Brests and Ruddy Cheeks; which they should love
moreover for being GODs Image, Queen of the Univers, Beloved
by Angels, Redeemed by Jesus Christ, an Heires of Heaven, and
Temple of the Holy Ghost: a Mine and fountain of all Vertues, a   10
Treasurie of Graces, and a Child of GOD. But these Excellencies
are unknown. They lov her perhaps, but do not lov God more: nor
Men as much: nor Heaven and Earth at all. And so being Defectiv
to other Things, perish by a seeming Excess to that. We should
be all Life and Mettle and Vigor and Lov to evry Thing. And that   15
would Poys us. I dare Confidently say, that evry Person in the
Whole World ought to be Beloved as much as this: And she if
there be any caus of Difference more then she is. But GOD being
Beloved infinitly more, will be infinitly more our Joy, and our
Heart will be more with Him. So that no Man can be in Danger   20
by loving others too much, that loveth GOD as He ought.

The Third Century

1

Will you see the Infancy of this sublime and celestial Greatness?
Those Pure and Virgin Apprehensions I had from the Womb, and
that Divine Light wherewith I was born, are the Best unto this
Day, wherin I can see the Universe. By the Gift of GOD they
5 attended me into the World, and by his Special favor I remember
them till now. Verily they seem the Greatest Gifts His Wisdom
could bestow · for without them all other Gifts had been Dead
and Vain. They are unattainable by Book, and therfore I will teach
them by Experience. Pray for them earnestly: for they will make
10 you Angelical, and wholy Celestial. Certainly Adam in Paradice
had not more sweet and Curious Apprehensions of the World,
then I when I was a child.

2

All appeared New, and Strange at the first, inexpressibly rare, and
Delightfull, and Beautifull. I was a little Stranger which at my
Enterance into the World was Saluted and Surrounded with
innumerable Joys. My Knowledg was Divine: I knew by Intuition
5 those things which since my Apostasie, I Collected again, by the
Highest Reason. My very Ignorance was Advantageous. I seemed
as one Brought into the Estate of Innocence. All Things were
Spotles and Pure and Glorious: yea, and infinitly mine, and Joyfull
and Precious. I knew not that there were any Sins, or Complaints,
10 or Laws. I Dreamed not of Poverties Contentions or Vices. All
Tears and Quarrels, were hidden from mine Eys. Evry Thing was
at Rest, Free, and Immortal. I knew Nothing of Sickness or Death
or Exaction, in the Absence of these I was Entertained like an
Angel with the Works of GOD in their Splendor and Glory; I saw
15 all in the Peace of Eden; Heaven and Earth did sing my Creators
Praises, and could not make more Melody to Adam, then to me.
All Time was Eternity, and a Perpetual Sabbath. Is it not Strange,
that an Infant should be Heir of the World, and see those
Mysteries which the Books of the Learned never unfold?

3

The Corn was Orient and Immortal Wheat, which never should be reaped, nor was ever sown. I thought it had stood from Everlasting to Everlasting. The Dust and Stones of the Street were as Precious as GOLD. The Gates were at first the End of the World, The Green Trees when I saw them first through one of the Gates Transported and Ravished me; their Sweetnes and unusual Beauty made my Heart to leap, and almost mad with Extasie, they were such strange and Wonderfull Thing[s]: The Men! O what Venerable and Reverend Creatures did the Aged seem! Immortal Cherubims! And yong Men Glittering and Sparkling Angels and Maids strange Seraphick Pieces of Life and Beauty! Boys and Girles Tumbling in the Street, and Playing, were moving Jewels. I knew not that they were Born or should Die. But all things abided Eternaly as they were in their Proper Places. Eternity was Manifest in the Light of the Day, and som thing infinit Behind evry thing appeared: which talked with my Expectation and moved my Desire. The Citie seemed to stand in Eden, or to be Built in Heaven. The Streets were mine, the Temple was mine, the People were mine, their Clothes and Gold and Silver was mine, as much as their Sparkling Eys fair Skins and ruddy faces. The Skies were mine, and so were the Sun and Moon and Stars, and all the World was mine, and I the only Spectator and Enjoyer of it. I knew no Churlish Proprieties, nor Bounds nor Divisions: but all Proprieties and Divisions were mine: all Treasures and the Possessors of them. So that with much adoe I was corrupted; and made to learn the Dirty Devices of this World. Which now I unlearn, and becom as it were a little Child again, that I may enter into the Kingdom of GOD.

5

Our Saviors Meaning, when He said, He must be Born again and becom a little Child that will enter into the Kingdom of Heaven: is Deeper far then is generaly believed. It is not only in a Careless Reliance upon Divine Providence, that we are to becom Little

Orient, radiant as dawn, lustrous; *Proprieties*, properties or possessions

5 Children, or in the feebleness and shortness of our Anger and
Simplicity of our Passions: but in the Peace and Purity of all our
Soul. Which Purity also is a Deeper Thing then is commonly
apprehended · for we must disrobe our selvs of all fals Colors, and
unclothe our Souls of evil Habits; all our Thoughts must be
10 Infant-like and Clear: the Powers of our Soul free from the Leven
of this World, and disentangled from mens conceits and customs.
Grit in the Ey or the yellow Jandice will not let a Man see those
Objects truly that are before it. And therfore it is requisit that we
should be as very Strangers to the Thoughts Customs and
15 Opinions of men in this World as if we were but little Children.
So those Things would appear to us only which do to Children
when they are first Born. Ambitions, Trades, Luxuries, inordinat
Affections, Casual and Accidental Riches invented since the fall
would be gone, and only those Things appear, which did to Adam
20 in Paradice, in the same Light, and in the same Colors. GOD in
His Works, Glory in the Light, Lov in our Parents, Men, our selvs,
and the Face of Heaven. Evry Man naturaly seeing those Things,
to the Enjoyment of which He is Naturaly Born.

6

Evry one provideth Objects, but few prepare Senses wherby, and
Light wherin to see them. Since therfore we are Born to be a
Burning and Shining Light, and whatever men learn of others,
they see in the Light of others Souls: I will in the Light of my Soul
5 shew you the Univers. Perhaps it is Celestial, and will teach you
how Beneficial we may be to each other. I am sure it is a Sweet
and Curious Light to me: which had I wanted: I would hav given
all the Gold and Silver in all Worlds to hav Purchased. But it was
the Gift of GOD and could not be bought with Mony. And by
10 what Steps and Degrees I proceeded to that Enjoyment of all
Eternity which now I possess I will likewise shew you. A Clear,
and familiar Light it may prove unto you.

7

The first Light which shined in my Infancy in its Primitive and
Innocent Clarity was totaly Ecclypsed: insomuch that I was fain

to learn all again. If you ask me how it was Ecclypsed? Truly by
the Customs and maners of Men, which like Contrary Winds
blew it out: by an innumerable company of other Objects, rude 5
vulgar and Worthless Things that like so many loads of Earth and
Dung did over whelm and Bury it: by the Impetuous Torrent of
Wrong Desires in all others whom I saw or knew that carried me
away and alienated me from it: by a Whole Sea of other Matters
and Concernments that Covered and Drowned it: finaly by the 10
Evil Influence of a Bad Education that did not foster and cherish
it. All Mens thoughts and Words were about other Matters; They
all prized New Things which I did not dream of. I was a stranger
and unacquainted with them; I was little and reverenced their
Authority; I was weak, and easily guided by their Example: 15
Ambitious also, and Desirous to approve my self unto them. And
finding no one Syllable in any mans Mouth of those Things, by
Degrees they vanishd, My Thoughts, (as indeed what is more
fleeting then a Thought) were blotted out. And at last all the
Celestial Great and Stable Treasures to which I was born, as wholy 20
forgotten, as if they had never been.

8

Had any man spoken of it, it had been the most easy Thing in the
World, to hav taught me, and to hav made me believ, that Heaven
and Earth was GODs Hous, and that He gav it me. That the Sun
was mine and that Men were mine, and that Cities and Kingdoms
were mine also: that Earth was better then Gold, and that Water 5
was, every Drop of it, a Precious Jewel. And that these were Great
and Living Treasures: and that all Riches whatsoever els was Dross
in Comparison. From whence I clearly find how Docible our
Nature is, in natural Things, were it rightly entreated. And that our
Misery proceedeth ten thousand times more from the outward 10
Bondage of Opinion and Custom, then from any inward
corruption or Depravation of Nature: And that it is not our Parents
Loyns, so much as our Parents lives, that Enthrals and Blinds us. Yet
is all our Corruption Derived from Adam: inasmuch as all the Evil

Docible, tractable, teachable

15 Examples and inclinations of the World arise from His Sin. But I
speak it in the presence of GOD and of our Lord Jesus Christ, in
my Pure Primitive Virgin Light, while my Apprehensions were
natural, and unmixed, I can not remember, but that I was ten
thousand times more prone to Good and Excellent Things, then
20 evil. But I was quickly tainted and fell by others.

9

It was a Difficult matter to persuade me that the Tinsild Ware
upon a Hobby hors was a fine thing. They did impose upon me,
and Obtrude their Gifts that made me believ a Ribban or a
Feather Curious. I could not see where the Curiousness or
5 fineness: And to Teach me that A Purs of Gold was of any valu
seemed impossible, the Art by which it becomes so, and the
reasons for which it is accounted so were so Deep and Hidden to
my Inexperience. So that Nature is still nearest to Natural Things
· and farthest off from preternatural, and to esteem that the
10 Reproach of Nature, is an Error in them only who are
unacquainted with it. Natural Things are Glorious, and to know
them Glorious: But to call things preternatural, Natural,
Monstrous. Yet all they do it, who esteem Gold Silver Houses
Lands Clothes &c. the Riches of Nature, which are indeed the
15 Riches of Invention. Nature knows no such Riches · but Art and
Error makes them. Not the God of Nature, but Sin only was the
Parent of them. The Riches of Nature are our Souls and Bodies,
with all their Faculties Sences and Endowments. And it had been
the Easiest thing in the whole World, that all felicity consisted in
20 the Enjoyment of all the World, that it was prepared for me before
I was born, and that Nothing was more Divine and Beautifull.

10

Thoughts are the most Present things to Thoughts, and of the
most Powerfull Influence. My Soul was only Apt and Disposed to
Great Things; But Souls to Souls are like Apples to Apples, one
being rotten rots another. When I began to speak and goe   ·

---

preternatural, unnatural

Nothing began to be present to me, but what was present in their
Thoughts. Nor was any thing present to me any other way, then
it was so to them. The Glass of Imagination was the only Mirror,
wherin any thing was represented or appeared to me. All Things
were Absent which they talkt not of. So I began among my Play
fellows to prize a Drum, a fine Coat, a Peny, a Gilded Book &c.
who before never Dreamd of any such Wealth. Goodly Objects to
drown all the Knowledg of Heaven and Earth: As for the Heavens
and the Sun and Stars they disappeared, and were no more unto
me than the bare Walls. So that the Strange Riches of Mans
Invention quite overcame the Riches of Nature. Being learned
more laboriously and in the second place.

11

By this let Nurses, and those Parents that desire Holy Children
learn to make them Possessors of Heaven and Earth betimes · to
remove silly Objects from before them, to Magnify nothing but
what is Great indeed, and to talk of God to them and of His
Works and Ways before they can either Speak or go. For Nothing
is so Easy as to teach the Truth becaus the Nature of the Thing
confirms the Doctrine. As when we say The Sun is Glorious, A
Man is a Beautifull Creature, Soveraign over Beasts and Fowls and
Fishes, The Stars Minister unto us, The World was made for you,
&c. But to say This Hous is yours, and these Lands are another
Mans and this Bauble is a Jewel and this Gugaw a fine Thing, this
Rattle makes Musick &c. is deadly Barbarous and uncouth to a
little Child; and makes him suspect all you say, becaus the Nature
of the Thing contradicts your Words. Yet doth that Blot out all
Noble and Divine Ideas, Dissettle his foundation, render him
uncertain in all Things, and Divide him from GOD. To teach him
those Objects are little vanities, and that tho GOD made them, by
the Ministery of Man, yet Better and more Glorious Things are
more to be Esteemed, is Natural and Easy.

12

By this you may see who are the Rude and Barbarous Indians. For
verily there is no Salvage Nation under the Cope of Heaven, that

is more absurdly Barbarous than the Christian World. They that go
Naked and Drink Water and liv upon Roots are like Adam, or
5 Angels in Comparison of us. But they indeed that call Beads and
Glass Buttons Jewels, and Dress them selvs with feather, and buy
pieces of Brass and broken hafts of Knives of our Merchants are
som what like us. But We pass them in Barbarous Opinions, and
Monstrous Apprehensions: which we Nick Name Civility, and the
10 Mode, amongst us. I am sure those Barbarous People that go
naked, com nearer to Adam God and Angels: in the Simplicity of
their Wealth, tho not in Knowledg.

13

You would not think how these Barbarous Inventions spoyle your
Knowledg. They put Grubs and Worms in Mens Heads: that are
Enemies to all Pure and True Apprehensions, and eat out all their
Happines. They make it impossible for them, in whom they reign,
5 to believ there is any Excellency in the Works of GOD, or to taste
any Sweetness in the Nobility of Nature, or to Prize any Common,
tho never so Great a Blessing. They alienat men from the Life of
GOD, and at last make them to live without GOD in the World.
To liv the Life of GOD is to live to all the Works of GOD, and to
10 enjoy them in His Image · from which they are wholy Diverted that
follow fashions. Their fancies are corrupted with other Gingles.

14

Being Swallowed up therfore in the Miserable Gulph of idle talk
and worthless vanities, thenceforth I lived among Shadows, like a
Prodigal Son feeding upon Husks with Swine. A Comfortless
Wilderness full of Thorns and Troubles the World was, or wors: a
5 Waste Place covered with Idleness and Play, and Shops and
Markets and Taverns. As for Churches they were things I did not
understand. And Scholes were a Burden: so that there was nothing
in the World worth the having, or Enjoying, but my Game and
Sport, which also was a Dream and being passed wholy forgotten.
10 So that I had utterly forgotten all Goodness Bounty Comfort and
Glory: which things are the very Brightness of the Glory of
GOD: for lack of which therfore He was unknown.

15

Yet somtimes in the midst of these Dreams, I should com a litle
to my self · so far as to feel I wanted som thing, secretly to
Expostulate with GOD for not giving me Riches, to long after an
unknown Happiness, to griev that the World was so Empty, and
to be dissatisfied with my present State becaus it was vain and   5
forlorn. I had heard of Angels, and much admired that here upon
earth nothing should be but Dirt and Streets and Gutters · for as
for the Pleasures that were in Great Mens Houses I had not seen
them: and it was my real Happiness they were unknown · for
becaus Nothing Deluded me, I was the more Inquisitive.   10

16

Once I remember (I think I was about 4 yeer old, when) I thus
reasoned with my self · sitting in a little Obscure Room in my
Fathers poor House. If there be a God, certainly He must be
infinit in Goodness. And that I was prompted to, by a real
Whispering Instinct of Nature. And if He be infinit in Goodness,   5
and a Perfect Being in Wisdom and Love, certainly He must do
most Glorious Things: and giv us infinit Riches; how comes it to
pass therfore that I am so poor? of so Scanty and Narrow a
fortune, enjoying few and Obscure Comforts? I thought I could
not believ Him a GOD to me, unless all His Power were Employd   10
to Glorify me. I knew not then my Soul, or Body: nor did I think
of the Heavens and the Earth, the Rivers and the Stars, the Sun
or the Seas: all those were lost, and Absent from me. But when I
found them made out of Nothing for me, then I had a GOD
indeed, whom I could Prais, and rejoyce in.   15

22

These Liquid Clear Satisfactions, were the Emanations of the
Highest Reason, but not atchieved till a long time afterwards. In
the mean time I was som times tho seldom visited and inspired
with New and more vigorous Desires after that Bliss which
Nature Whispered and Suggested to me. Evry New Thing   5
Quickened my Curiosity and raised my Expectation. I remember
once, the first time I came into a Magnificent or Noble Dining

Room, and was left there alone, I rejoyced to see the Gold and
State and Carved Imagery · but when all was Dead, and there was
10 no Motion, I was weary of it, and departed Dissatisfied. But
afterwards, when I saw it full of Lords and Ladies and Musick and
Dancing, the Place which once seemed not to differ from a
Solitary Den, had now Entertainment and nothing of Tediousness
but pleasure in it. By which I perceived (upon a Reflexion made
15 long after) That Men and Women are when well understood a
Principal Part of our True felicity. By this I found also that
nothing that stood still, could by doing so be a Part of Happiness:
and that Affection, tho it were invisible, was the best of Motions.
But the August and Glorious Exercise of Virtue, was more
20 Solemn and Divine which yet I saw not. And that all Men and
Angels should appear in Heaven.

23

Another time, in a Lowering and sad Evening, being alone in the
field, when all things were dead and quiet, a certain Want and
Horror fell upon me, beyond imagination. The unprofitableness
and Silence of the Place dissatisfied me, its Wideness terrified me,
5 from the utmost Ends of the Earth fears surrounded me. How did
I know but Dangers might suddainly arise from the East, and
invade me from the unknown Regions beyond the Seas? I was a
Weak and little child, and had forgotten there was a man alive in
the Earth. Yet som thing also of Hope and Expectation comforted
10 me from every Border. This taught me that I was concernd in all
the World: and that in the remotest Borders the Causes of Peace
delight me, and the Beauties of the Earth when seen were made
to entertain me: that I was made to hold a Communion with the
Secrets of Divine Providence in all the World: that a
15 Remembrance of all the Joys I had from my Birth ought always
to be with me: that the Presence of Cities Temples and Kingdoms
ought to Sustain me, and that to be alone in the World was to be
Desolate and Miserable. The Comfort of Houses and friends, and
the clear Assurance of Treasures evry where, Gods Care and Lov,
20 His Goodnes Wisdom and Power, His presence and Watchfulness
in all the Ends of the Earth, were my Strength and Assurance for

ever: and that these things being Absent to my Ey, were my Joys
and consolations: as present to my Understanding as the Wideness
and Emptiness of the Universe which I saw before me.

The Fourth Century

13

One great Discouragement to Felicity, or rather to great Souls in
the persuit of Felicity, is the Solitariness of the Way that leadeth to
her Temple. A man that studies Happiness must sit alone like a
Sparrow upon the Hous Top, and like a Pelican in the Wilderness.
And the reason is becaus all men prais Happiness and despise it · 5
very few shall a Man find in the way of Wisdom: And few indeed
that having given up their Names to Wisdom and felicity, that will
persevere in seeking it. Either He must go on alone, or go back for
company. People are tickled with the Name of it, and som are
persuaded to Enterprize a little, but quickly draw back when they 10
see the trouble, yea cool of them selvs without any Trouble. Those
Mysteries which while men are Ignorant of, they would giv all the
Gold in the World for, I hav seen when Known to be despised. Not
as if the Nature of Happiness were such that it did need a vail: but
the Nature of Man is such, that it is Odious and ingratefull. For 15
those things which are most Glorious when most Naked, are by
Men when most Nakedly reveald most Despised. So that GOD is
fain for His very Names sake, lest His Beauties should be scorned
to conceal her Beauties: and for the sake of Men, which naturaly
are more prone to prie into secret and forbidden things then into 20
Open and common. Felicity is amiable under a Vail, but most
Amiable when most Naked. It hath its times, and seasons for both.
There is som Pleasure in breaking the Shell: and many Delights in
our Addresses, previous to the Sweets in the Possession of her. It is
som Part of Felicity that we must seek her. 25

14

In order to this, he furnished him self with this Maxime. *It is a*
Good Thing to be Happy alone. It is better to be Happy in

Company, but Good to be Happy alone. Men owe me the Advantage of their Society, but if they deny me that just Debt, I will not be unjust to my self, and side with them in bereaving me. I will not be Discouraged, least I be Miserable for Company. More Company increases Happiness, but does not leighten or Diminish Misery.

27

He conceived it his Duty and much Delighted in the Obligation; That he was to treat evry Man in the whole World as the Representativ of Mankind, And that he was to meet in him, and to Pay unto Him all the Lov of God Angels and Men.

29

He had another saying, He lives most like an Angel that lives upon least Himself, and doth most Good to others. For the Angels neither eat nor Drink, and yet do Good to the whole World. Now a Man is an Incarnat Angel. And He that lives in the midst of Riches as a poor man Himself, Enjoying God and Paradice, or Christendom which is Better, conversing with the Poor, and seeing the valu of their Souls through their Bodies, and prizing all things cleerly with a due esteem, is arrived here to the Estate of Immortality. He cares little for the Delicacies either of food or Raiment himself: and Delighteth in others. God Angels and Men are his Treasures. He seeth through all the Mists and Vails of Invention, and possesseth here beneath the true Riches. And he that doth this always, is a rare Phoenix: But he confessed that he had often caus to bewail his Infirmities.

30

I speak not His Practices but His Principles. I should too much Prais your friend did I speak his Practices, but it is no shame for any man to declare his Principles, tho they are the most Glorious in the world. Rather they are to be Shamed that have no Glorious Principles: or that are ashamed of them. This he desired me to tell you becaus of Modesty. But with all, that indeed his Practices are so short of these Glorious Principles, that to relate them would be

to his Shame; and that therfore you would never look upon him
but as clothed in the Righteousness of Jesus Christ. Nevertheless
I hav heard him often say, That he never allowd himself in   10
Swerving from any of these. And that he repented deeply of evry
Miscarriage: and moreover firmly resolved as much as was possible
never to erre or wander from them again.

31

I heard him often say that Holiness and Happiness were the same
and he coated a mighty Place of Scripture, All her ways are
pleasantness and her Paths are Peace. But he delighted in giving the
Reason of Scripture, and therfore said, That Holiness and Wisdom
in Effect were one · for no man could be Wise that Knew Excellent   5
Things, without doing them. Now to do them is Holiness, and to
do them Wisdom. No man therfore can be further Miserable then
he swerveth from the Ways of Holiness and Wisdom.

32

If he might hav had but one Request of GOD Almighty it should
hav been abov all other, that he might be a Blessing to Mankind.
That was his Daily Prayer abov all his Petitions. He wisely knew
that it included all Petitions · for He that is a Blessing to Mankind
must be Blessed, that he may be so, and must inherit all their   5
Affections and in that their Treasures. He could not Help it. But
he so desired to lov them, and to be a Joy unto them, that he
protested often, that He could never Enjoy Himself, but as He was
enjoyed of others, and that above all Delights in all Worlds, he
desired to be a Joy and Blessing to others. Tho for this he was not   10
to be commended, for he did but Right to God and Nature, who
had implanted in all that Inclination.

33

The desire of Riches was removed from Himself pretty Early. He
often Protested, If he had a Palace of Gold and a Paradice of
Delights, besides that he enjoyed, he could not understand a

Miscarriage, mishandling or misbehaviour; *coated*, quoted

farthing worth of Benefit that he should receiv therby, unless in
giving it away · but for others he somtimes could desire Riches ·
till at last perceiving that Root of Covetousness in Him, and that
it would grow as long as it was Shrouded under that Mould: He
rooted it quite up with this Principle. *Somtimes it may so Happen,*
that to contemn the World in the Whole Lump, was as Acceptable to
GOD as first to get it with solicitud and care, and then to retail it out in
Particular Charities.

34

After this he could say with Luther, that Covetousness could
never fasten the least hold upon Him. And concerning his friends
even to the very Desire of seeing them rich, he could say as
Phocion the Poor Athenian did of his children. Either they will
be like, me or not, if they are like me they will not need Riches,
if they are not they will be but needless and Hurtfull Superfluities.

35

He desired no other Riches for his friends, but those which
cannot be Abused: to wit the True Treasures, God and Heaven and
Earth and Angels and Men, &c. with the Riches of Wisdom and
Grace to enjoy them. And it was his Principle That all the
Treasures in the whole World would not make a Miser Happy. A
Miser is not only a Covetous Man but a fool. Any Needy Man,
that wanteth the World, is Miserable. He wanteth God and all
Things.

36

He thought also that no Poverty could befall him that enjoyd
Paradice · for when all the Things are gone which Men can giv,
A Man is still as Rich as Adam was in Eden: who was Naked
there. A Naked Man is the Richest Creature in all Worlds: and can
never be Happy; till he sees the Riches of his Nakedness. He is
very Poor in Knowledg that thinks Adam poor in Eden. See here
how one Principle helps another. All our Disadvantages
contracted by the fall are made up and recompensed by the Lov
of God.

37

Tis not Change of Place, but Glorious Principles well Practiced
that establish Heaven in the Life and Soul. An Angel will be
Happy any where; and a Divel Miserable. Becaus the Principles of
the one are always Good, of the other Bad · from the Centre to
the utmost Bounds of the Everlasting Hills, all is Heaven before   5
God, and full of Treasure. And he that walks like God in the midst
of them, Blessed.

48

By this you may see, that the Works or Actions flowing from your
own Liberty are of Greater Concernment to you then all that
could possibly happen besides. And that it is more to your
Happiness what you are, then what you enjoy. Should God giv
him self and all Worlds to you, and you refuse them, it would be   5
to no purpose · should he lov you and magnify you, should he giv
his Son to Dy for you and command all Angels and Men to lov
you, should he Exalt you in his Throne, and giv you Dominion
over all his Works and you neglect them it would be to no
purpose. Should he make you in his Image, and employ all his   10
Wisdom and Power to fill Eternity with Treasures, and you despise
them it would be in vain. In all these Things you hav to do; and
therfore your Actions are great and Magnificent, being of infinit
Importance in all Eys. While all Creatures stand in Expectation
what will be the result of your Liberty. Your Exterior Works are   15
little in Comparison of these. And God infinitly desires you
should demean your self Wisely in these Affairs: that is Rightly.
Esteeming and receiving what he gives, with Veneration and Joy
and infinit Thanksgiving. Many other Works there are, but this is
the Great Work of all Works to be performed. Consider Whether   20
more depends upon Gods Lov to you, or your Lov to Him. From
His Lov all the Things in Heaven and Earth flow unto you; but if
you lov neither Him nor them, you bereav your self of all, and
make them infinitly evil and Hurtfull to you and your self
abominable. So that upon your Lov naturaly depends your own   25
Excellency and the Enjoyment of His. It is by your Lov that you
enjoy all His Delights, and are Delightfull to Him.

55

He was a Strict and Severe Applier of all Things to Himself. And would first hav his Self Lov satisfied, and then his Lov of all others. It is true that Self Lov is Dishonorable, but then it is when it is alone. And Self endedness is Mercinary, but then it is when it
5 endeth in oneself. It is more Glorious to lov others, and more desirable, but by Natural Means to be attained. That Pool must first be filled, that shall be made to overflow. He was ten yeers studying before he could satisfy his Self Lov. And now finds nothing more easy then to lov others better than oneself. And that to love
10 Mankind so is the comprehensiv Method to all felicity. For it makes a Man Delightfull to GOD and Men, to Himself and Spectators, and God and Men Delightfull to Him, and all creatures infinitly in them. But as not to lov oneself at all is Bruitish: or rather Absurd and Stonish: (for Beasts do lov themselvs) so hath GOD by rational
15 Methods enabled us to lov others better then our selvs, and therby made us the most Glorious Creatures. Had we not loved our selvs at all we could never hav been obliged to lov any thing. So that self Lov is the Basis of all Lov. But when we do Lov our selvs, and self Lov is satisfied infinitly in all its Desires and possible Demands, then
20 it is easily led to regard the Benefactor more then it self, and for his sake overflows abundantly to all others. So that God by satisfying my self Lov, hath enabled, and engaged me to love others.

56

No man loves, but he loves another more then Himself. In mean Instances this is apparent. If you com into an Orchard with a person you lov, and there be but one ripe cherry you prefer it to the other. If two lovers Delight in the same piece of Meat, either takes pleasure in
5 the other, and more esteems the Beloveds Satisfaction. What ailes men, that they do not see it? In greater Cases this is Evident. A mother runs upon a sword to save her Beloved. A Father leaps into the fire to fetch out his Beloved. Lov brought Christ from Heaven to Die for his Beloved. It is in the Nature of Lov to Despise it self:
10 and to think only of its Beloveds Welfare. Look to it, it is not right Lov, that is otherwise. Moses and S. Paul were no fools. God make me one of their Number. I am sure Nothing is more Acceptable to

him, then to lov others so as to be willing to impart even ones own Soul for their Benefit and welfare.

93

Our Friendship with God ought to be so Pure and so Clear, that Nakedly and Simply for his Divine Lov, for his Glorious Works and Blessed Laws, the Wisdom of His Counsels, his Ancient Ways and Attributs towards us, we should ever in Publick endeavor to Honor Him. Always taking care to Glorify Him before Men: to Speak of His Goodness, to Sanctify His Name, and do those Things that will stir up others, and occasion others to Glorify Him. Doing this so Zealously, that we would not forbear the least Act wherin we might serv Him for all Worlds. It ought to be a firm Principle rooted in us, that this Life is the most precious Season in all Eternity, becaus all Eternity dependeth on it. Now we may do those Actions which herafter we shall never hav occasion to do. And now we are to do them in another maner, which in its place is the most Acceptable in all Worlds · namely by Faith and Hope, in which God infinitly Delighteth. With Difficulty and Danger, which God infinitly commiserats, and Greatly esteems. So piecing this Life with the life of Heaven, and seeing it as one with all Eternity · a Part of it, a Life within it. Strangely and Stupendiously Blessed in its Place and Season.

94

Having once studied these Principles you are Eternaly to Practice them. You are to warm your self at these fires, and to hav recours to them evry Day. When you think not of these Things you are in the Dark. And if you would walk in the Light of them, you must frequently Meditat. These Principles are like Seed in the Ground, they must continualy be visited with Heavenly Influences, or els your Life will be a Barren feild. Perhaps they might be cast into Better frame, and more Curiously Exprest; but if well Cultivated they will be as fruitfull, as if every Husk were a Golden Rinde. It is the Substance that is in them that is productive of Joy, and Good to all.

The Fifth Century

1

The objects of Felicitie, and the Way of enjoying them, are two Material Themes; wherin to be instructed is infinitly desirable, becaus as Necessary, as Profitable. Whether of the Two, the Object, or the Way be more Glorious; it is difficult to determine. God is the Object, and God is the Way of Enjoying. God in all his Excellencies, Laws and Works, in all his Ways and Counsels is the Sovereign Object of all Felicitie. Eternity and Time, Heaven and Earth, Kingdoms and Ages, Angels and Men, are in him to be enjoyed. In him, the fountain, in him the End; in him the Light, the Life, the Way, in him the Glory and Crown of all. Yet for Distinction sake, we will speak of several eminent Particulars. Beginning with his Attributes.

2

The Infinity of God is our Enjoyment, because it is the Region and Extent of his Dominion. Barely as it comprehends infinit Space, it is infinitly Delightfull; becaus it is the Room and the Place of our Treasures, the Repositorie of our Joys, and the Dwelling Place, yea the Sea and Throne, and Kingdom of our Souls. But as it is the Light wherin we see, the Life that inspires us, the Violence of his Love, and the Strength of our Enjoyments, the Greatness and Perfection of evry Creature, the Amplitude that enlargeth us, and the field wherin our Thoughts expaciate without Limit or Restraint, the Ground and Foundation of all our Satisfactions, the Operative Energie and Power of the Deitie, the Measure of our Delights, and the Grandure of our Souls, it is more our Treasure, and ought more abundantly to be delighted in. It surroundeth us continualy on evry side, it filles us, and inspires us. It is so Mysterious, that it is wholy within us, and even then it wholy seems, and is without us. It is more inevitably and constantly, more neerly and immediately our Dwelling Place, then our Cities and Kingdoms and houses. Our Bodies them selvs are

---

barely, merely

not so much ours, or within us as that is. The Immensitie of God
is an Eternal Tabernacle. Why then we should not be sensible of
that as much as of our Dwellings, I cannot tell, unless our
Corruption and Sensuality destroy us. We ought always to feel,
admire, and walk in it. It is more clearly objected to the Ey of the
Soul, then our Castles and Palaces to the Ey of the Body. Those
Accidental Buildings may be thrown down, or we may be taken 25
from them, but this can never be removed, it abideth for ever. It
is impossible not to [be] within it, nay to be so surrounded as
evermore to be in the centre and midst of it, wherever we can
possibly remov, is inevitably fatal to evry Being.

3

Creatures that are able to dart their Thoughts into all Spaces, can
brook no Limit or Restraint, they are infinitly endebted to this
illimited Extent, becaus were there no such Infinitie, there would
be no Room for their Imaginations; their Desires and Affections
would be coopd up, and their Souls imprisoned. We see the 5
Heavens with our Eys, and Know the World with our Sences. But
had we no Eys, nor Sences, we should see Infinitie like the Holy
Angels. The Place wherin the World standeth, were it all
annihilated would still remain, the Endless Extent of which we
feel so realy and palpably, that we do not more certainly know the 10
Distinctions and figures, and Bounds and Distances of what we
see, then the Everlasting Expansion of what we feel and behold
within us. It is an Object infinitly Great and Ravishing: as full of
Treasures as full of Room, and as fraught with Joy as Capacitie. To
Blind men it seemeth dark, but is all Glorious within, as infinit in 15
Light and Beauty, as Extent and Treasure. Nothing is in vain, much
less Infinity. Evry Man is alone the Centre and Circumference of
it. It is all his own, and so Glorious, that it is the Eternal and
Incomprehensible Essence of the Deitie. A Cabinet of infinit Value
equal in Beauty Lustre and Perfection to all its Treasures. It is the 20
Bosom of God, the Soul and Securitie of every Creature.

fatal, of fate, destined

4

Were it not for this Infinitie, Gods Bountie would of Necessitie
be limited. His Goodness would want a Receptacle for its
Effusions. His Gifts would be confined into Narrow Room, and
his Almighty Power for lack of a Theatre Magnificent enough, a
5 Storehouse large enough be Straitned. But Almighty Power
includes Infinitie in its own Existence. For becaus God is infinitly
able to do all Things, there must of Necessity be an infinit
Capacitie to answer that Power, becaus Nothing it self is an
Obedient Subject to work upon: and the Eternal Privation of
10 infinit Perfections is to almighty Power a Being Capable of all. As
sure as there is a Space infinit, there is a Power, a Bounty, a
Goodness, a Wisdom infinit, a Treasure, a Blessedness, a Glory.

5

Infinity of Space is like a Painters Table, prepared for the Ground
and feild of those Colors that are to be laid theron. Look how
great he intends the Picture, so Great doth he make the Table. It
would be an Absurditie to leav it unfinished, or not to fill it. To
5 leav any part of it Naked and bare, and void of Beauty, would
render the whole ungratefull to the Ey, and argue a Defect of
Time, or Materials, or Wit in the Limner. As the Table is infinit so
are the Pictures. Gods Wisdom is the Art, his Goodness the Will,
his Word the Penicill, his Beauty and Power the Colors, his
10 Pictures are all his Works and Creatures · infinitly more Real, and
more Glorious, as well as more Great and Manifold then the
Shadows of a Landschape. But the Life of all is, they are the
Spectators own. He is in them as in his Territories, and in all these,
views his own Possessions.

6

One would think that besides infinit Space there could be no
more Room for any Treasure. Yet to shew that God is infinitly
infinit, there is Infinit Room besides, and perhaps a more
Wonderfull Region making this to be infinitly infinit. No man

Painters Table, tablet, canvas

will believ that besides the Space from the Centre of the Earth to the utmost bounds of the Everlasting Hills, there should be any more. Beyond those Bounds perhaps there may, but besides all that Space that is illimited and present before us, and absolutly endles evry Way, where can there be any Room for more? This is the Space that is at this Moment only present before our Ey, the only Space that was, or that will be, from Everlasting to Everlasting. This Moment Exhibits infinit Space, but there is a Space also wherin all Moments are infinitly Exhibited, and the Everlasting Duration of infinit Space is another Region and Room of Joys. Wherin all Ages appear together, all Occurrences stand up at once, and the innumerable and Endless Myriads of yeers that were before the Creation, and will be after the World is ended are Objected as a Clear and Stable Object, whose several Parts extended out at length, giv an inward Infinity to this Moment, and compose an Eternitie that is seen by all Comprehensors and Enjoyers.

7

Eternity is a Mysterious Absence of Times and Ages: an Endless Length of Ages always present, and for ever Perfect. For as there is an immovable Space wherin all finit Spaces are enclosed, and all Motions carried on, and performed: so is there an Immovable Duration, that contains and measures all moving Durations. Without which first the last could not be; no more then finit Places, and Bodies moving without infinit Space. All Ages being but successions correspondent to those Parts of that Eternitie wherin they abide, and filling no more of it, then Ages can do. Whether they are commensurat with it or no, is difficult to determine. But the infinit immovable Duration is Eternitie, the Place and Duration of all Things, even of Infinit Space it self: the Cause and End, the Author and Beautifier, the Life and Perfection of all.

8

Eternitie magnifies our Joys exceedingly · for wheras things in them selvs began, and quickly end · Before they came, were never in Being; do service but for few Moments; and after they are gone, pass away and leav us for ever · Eternity retains the Moments of their Beginning and Ending within it self: and from Everlasting to Everlasting those Things were in their Times and Places before God, and in all their Circumstances Eternaly will be, serving him in those Moments wherin they existed, to those Intents and Purposes for which they were Created. The Swiftest Thought is present with him Eternaly: the Creation and the Day of Judgement, his first Consultation Choise and Determination, the Result and End of all just now in full Perfection, ever Beginning, ever Passing, ever Ending: with all the Intervalles of Space between things and Things. As if those Objects that arise many thousand yeers one after the other were all together. We also were our selvs before God Eternaly: And hav the Joy of seeing our selvs Eternaly beloved, and Eternaly Blessed, and infinitly Enjoying all the Parts of our Blessedness, in all the Durations of Eternity appearing at once before our selvs, when perfectly Consummat in the Kingdom of Light and Glory. The Smallest Thing by the Influence of Eternity, is made infinit and Eternal. We pass thorow a standing Continent or Region of Ages, that are already before us, Glorious and perfect while we com to them. Like men in a ship we pass forward, the shores and Marks seeming to go backward, tho we move, and they stand still. We are not with them in our Progressive Motion, but prevent the Swiftness of our Course, and are present with them in our Understandings. Like the Sun we dart our Rayes before us, and occupy those Spaces with Light and Contemplation, which we move towards, but possess not with our Bodies. And seeing all Things in the Light of Divine Knowledg eternaly serving God, rejoyce unspeakably in that service, and enjoy it all.

prevent, precede, go before

Selected Poems and *Thanksgivings*

The poems that follow in this section come mainly from two sources, the Dobell Manuscript, which Traherne collated himself, and the Burney Manuscript, which was altered by Traherne's brother Philip. These poems develop the familiar themes of early innocence, the infinite capacity of the soul, felicity and desire as an engine towards felicity. The poems from the Dobell Manuscript are best read as a sequence rather than as a collection of unrelated poems. However, in order to allow room in the anthology for hitherto unpublished work, and for a taste from the *Thanksgivings*, neither the Dobell nor the Burney sequence of poems is presented in full here. I can only hope that what is lost in breaking the sequence may be made up for by the thrill of new discovery.

The last two pieces, a long stanza and the final fragment from the newly discovered unfinished poem *The Ceremonial Law*, outline the human reaction to the display of divine glory in a most tantalizingly unfinished manner. Moses descending from Mount Sinai is at once too glorious to be seen and the very object that draws the eyes of all. Himself untouched, he seems untouchable while all he touches is transformed and all they cannot touch allures.

From the Dobell Manuscript

The Salutation

1
These little Limmes,
These Eys and Hands which here I find,
These rosie Cheeks wherwith my Life begins,
Where have ye been,? Behind
5   What Curtain were ye from me hid so long!
Where was? in what Abyss, my Speaking Tongue?

2
When silent I,
So many thousand thousand yeers,
Beneath the Dust did in a Chaos lie,
10   How could I Smiles or Tears,
Or Lips or Hands or Eys or Ears perceiv?
Welcom ye Treasures which I now receiv.

3
I that so long
Was Nothing from Eternitie,
15   Did little think such Joys as Ear or Tongue,
To Celebrat or See:
Such Sounds to hear, such Hands to feel, such Feet,
Beneath the Skies, on such a Ground to meet.

4
New Burnisht Joys!
20   Which yellow Gold and Pearl excell!
Such Sacred Treasures are the Lims in Boys,
In which a Soul doth Dwell;
Their Organized Joynts, and Azure Veins
More Wealth include, then all the World contains.

5

From Dust I rise,   25
And out of Nothing now awake,
These Brighter Regions which salute mine Eys,
      A Gift from GOD I take.
The Earth, the Seas, the Light, the Day, the Skies,
The Sun and Stars are mine; if those I prize.   30

6

Long time before
I in my Mothers Womb was born,
A GOD preparing did this Glorious Store,
      The World for me adorne.
Into this Eden so Divine and fair,   35
So Wide and Bright, I com his Son and Heir.

7

A Stranger here
Strange Things doth meet, Strange Glories See;
Strange Treasures lodg'd in this fair World appear,
      Strange all, and New to me.   40
But that they mine should be, who nothing was,
That Strangest is of all, yet brought to pass.

My Spirit

1

My Naked Simple Life was I.
      That Act so Strongly Shind
Upon the Earth, the Sea, the Skie,
      It was the Substance of My Mind.
      The Sence it self was I.   5
I felt no Dross nor Matter in my Soul,
No Brims nor Borders, such as in a Bowl
We see, My Essence was Capacitie.
      That felt all Things,

10   The Thought that Springs
Therfrom's it self. It hath no other Wings
To Spread abroad, nor Eys to see,
Nor Hands Distinct to feel,
Nor Knees to Kneel:
15   But being Simple like the Deitie
In its own Centre is a Sphere
Not shut up here, but evry Where.

2

It Acts not from a Centre to
Its Object as remote,
20   But present is, when it doth view,
Being with the Being it doth note.
Whatever it doth do,
It doth not by another Engine work,
But by it self; which in the Act doth lurk.
25   Its Essence is Transformd into a true
And perfect Act.
And so Exact
Hath God appeard in this Mysterious Fact,
That tis all Ey, all Act, all Sight,
30   And what it pleas can be,
Not only see,
Or do; for tis more Voluble then Light:
Which can put on ten thousand Forms,
Being clothd with what it self adorns.

3

35   This made me present evermore
With whatso ere I saw.
An Object, if it were before
My Ey, was by Dame Natures Law,
Within my Soul. Her Store
40   Was all at once within me; all her Treasures

Voluble, protean, variable, taking on many forms

Were my Immediat and Internal Pleasures,
Substantial Joys, which did inform my Mind.
   With all she wrought,
   My Soul was fraught,
And evry Object in my Soul a Thought   45
  Begot, or was; I could not tell,
   Whether the Things did there
   Themselvs appear,
Which in my Spirit *truly* seemd to dwell;
  Or whether my conforming Mind   50
  Were not alone even all that shind.

      4
  But yet of this I was most sure,
   That at the utmost Length,
   (so Worthy was it to endure)
  My Soul could best Express its Strength.   55
   It was so Indivisible and so Pure,
That all my Mind was wholy Evry where
What ere it saw, twas ever wholy there;
The Sun ten thousand Legions off, was nigh:
   The utmost Star,   60
   Tho seen from far,
Was present in the Apple of my Eye.
  There was my Sight, my Life, my Sence,
   My Substance and my Mind
   My Spirit Shind   65
Even there, not by a Transeunt Influence.
  The Act was Immanent, yet there.
  The Thing remote, yet felt even here.

---

conforming, forming, shaping; *Transeunt*, operating beyond itself, opposite to
immanent

5

O Joy! O Wonder, and Delight!
70   O Sacred Mysterie!
My Soul a Spirit infinit!
An Image of the Deitie!
    A pure Substantiall Light!
That Being Greatest which doth Nothing seem!
75 Why, twas my All, I nothing did esteem
But that alone. A Strange Mysterious Sphere!
    A Deep Abyss
    That sees and is
The only Proper Place or Bower of Bliss.
80   To its Creator tis so near
    In Lov and Excellence
    In Life and Sence,
In Greatness Worth and Nature; And so Dear;
    In it, without Hyperbole,
85   The Son and friend of God we see.

6

A Strange Extended Orb of Joy,
    Proceeding from within,
    Which did on evry side convey
    It self, and being nigh of Kin
90   To God did evry Way
Dilate it self even in an Instant, and
Like an Indivisible Centre Stand
At once Surrounding all Eternitie.
    Twas not a Sphere
95   Yet did appear
One infinit. Twas somwhat evry where.
    And tho it had a Power to see
    Far more, yet still it shind
    And was a Mind
100 Exerted for it saw Infinitie

Line 75, first comma an editorial insertion for clarity

Twas not a Sphere, but twas a Power
Invisible, and yet a Bower.

7

O Wondrous Self! O Sphere of Light,
  O Sphere of Joy most fair;
O Act, O Power infinit;   105
O Subtile, and unbounded Air!
  O Living Orb of Sight!
Thou which within me art, yet Me! Thou Ey,
And Temple of his Whole Infinitie!
O what a World art Thou! a World within!   110
    All Things appear,
    All Objects are
Alive in thee! Supersubstancial, Rare,
  Abov them selvs, and nigh of Kin
    To those pure Things we find   115
      In his Great Mind
Who made the World! tho now Ecclypsd by Sin.
  There thev are Usefull and Divine,
  Exalted there they ought to Shine.

The Circulation

1

As fair Ideas from the Skie,
  Or Images of Things,
Unto a Spotless Mirror flie,
  On unperceived Wings;
And lodging there affect the Sence,   5
  As if at first they came from thence;
While being there, they richly Beautifie
The Place they fill, and yet communicat
Themselvs, reflecting to the Seers Ey,

Ideas, forms, patterns, archetypes

10   Just such is our Estate.
No Prais can we return again,
No Glory in our selvs possess,
But what derived from without we gain,
From all the Mysteries of Blessedness.

2

15   No Man breaths out more vital Air,
Then he before suckt in.
Those Joys and Praises must repair
To us, which tis a Sin
To bury, in a Senceless Tomb.
20   An Earthly Wight must be the Heir
Of all those Joys, the Holy Angels Prize,
He must a King, before a Priest becom,
And Gifts receiv, or ever Sacrifice.
Tis Blindness Makes us Dumb.
25   Had we but those Celestial Eys,
Wherby we could behold the Sum
Of all his Bounties, *we should overflow*
With Praises, did we but their Causes Know.

3

All Things to Circulations owe
30   Themselvs; by which alone
They do exist: They cannot shew
A Sigh, a Word, a Groan,
A Colour, or a Glimps of Light,
The Sparcle of a Precious Stone,
35   A virtue, or a Smell; a lovly Sight,
A Fruit, a Beam, an Influence, a Tear;
But they anothers Livery must Wear:
And borrow Matter first,
Before they can communicat.
40   Whatever's empty is accurst:

Wight, a living being, a creature; '*or ever Sacrifice*', 'ere ever Sacrifice'

And this doth shew that we must some Estate
Possess, or never can communicate.

4

A Spunge drinks in that Water, which
Is afterwards *exprest*.
A Liberal hand must first be rich: 45
Who blesseth must be Blest.
The Thirsty Earth drinks in the Rain,
The Trees suck Moysture at their Roots,
Before the one can Lavish Herbs again,
Before the other can afford us Fruits.   50
No Tenant can rais Corn, or pay his Rent,
Nor can even hav a Lord,
That has no Land. No Spring can vent,
No vessel any Wine afford
Wherin no Liquor's put. No Empty Purs,   55
Can Pounds or Talents of it self disburs.

5

Flame that Ejects its Golden Beams,
Sups up the Grosser Air;
To Seas, that pour out their Streams
In Springs, those Streams repair;   60
Receivd Ideas make even Dreams.
No Fancy painteth foule or fair
But by the Ministry of Inward Light,
That in the Spirits Cherisheth its Sight.
The Moon returneth Light, and som men say   65
The very Sun no Ray
Nor Influence could hav, did it
No forrein Aids, no food admit.
The Earth no Exhalations would afford,
Were not its Spirits by the Sun restord.   70

6

All things do first receiv, that giv.
    Only tis GOD above,
That from, and in himself doth live,
    Whose All sufficient Love
75   Without Original can flow
And all the Joys and Glories shew
Which Mortal Man can take Delight to know.
He is the Primitive Eternal Spring
The Endless Ocean of each Glorious Thing.
80   The Soul a Vessel is
A Spacious Bosom to Contain
All the fair Treasures of his Bliss
Which run like Rivers from, into the Main,
And all it doth receiv returns again.

The Recovery

1

To see us but receiv, is such a Sight
As makes his Treasures infinit!
Becaus His Goodness doth possess
In us, His own, and our own Blessedness.
5   Yea more, His Love doth take Delight
To make our Glory Infinite
        Our Blessedness to see
        Is even to the Deitie
A Beatifick Vision! He attains
10   His Ends while we enjoy. In us He reigns.

2

For God enjoyd is all his End.
Himself he then doth Comprehend.
When He is Blessed, Magnified,
Extold, Exalted, Praisd and Glorified

Honord, Esteemd, Belovd, Enjoyd,   15
Admired, Sanctified, Obeyd,
   That is receivd. For He
Doth place his Whole Felicitie
In that, who is despised and defied
Undeified almost if once denied.   20

3
In all his Works, in all his Ways,
We must his Glory see and Prais;
   And since our Pleasure is the End,
We must his Goodness and his Lov attend.
If we despise his Glorious Works,   25
Such Sin and Mischief in it lurks,
   That they are all made vain
   And this is even Endless Pain
To him that sees it. Whose Diviner Grief
Is hereupon (Ah me!) without relief.   30

4
We pleas his Goodness that receiv:
Refusers Him of all bereav.
As Bride grooms Know full well that Build
A Palace for their Bride. It will not yeeld
   Any Delight to him at all   35
   If She for whom He made the Hall
    Refuse to dwell in it
   Or Plainly Scorn the Benefit.
Her Act that 's Wo'ed, yeelds more delight and Pleasure
If she receivs, Then all that Pile of Treasure.   40

5
But we have Hands and Lips and Eys
And Hearts and Souls can Sacrifice.
   And Souls themselvs are made in vain
If we our Evil Stubbornness retain.
   Affections, Praises, are the Things   45

For which he gave us all these Springs,
They are the very fruits
Of all these Trees and Roots
The Fruits and Ends of all his Great Endeavors,
50   Which he abolisheth whoever Severs.

6
Tis not alone a Lively Sence
A clear and Quick Intelligence
A free, Profound, and full Esteem:
Tho these Elixars all and Ends to[o] seem
55   But Gratitude, Thanksgiving, Prais,
A Heart returnd for all these Joys,
These are the Things admird,
These are the Things by Him desird.
These are the Nectar and the Quintessence
60   The Cream and Flower that most affect his Sence.

7
The voluntary Act wherby
These are repaid, is in his Ey
More Precious then the very Skie.
All Gold and Silver is but Empty Dross
65   Rubies and Saphires are but Loss
The very Sun and Stars and Seas
Far less his Spirit pleas.
One Voluntary Act of Love
Far more Delightfull to his Soul doth prove
70   And is abov all these as far as Love.

Desire

1
For giving me Desire,
An Eager Thirst, a burning Ardent fire,
A virgin Infant Flame,

A Love with which into the World I came,
   An Inward Hidden Heavenly Love,   5
     Which in my Soul did Work and move,
     And ever ever me Enflame,
With restlesse longing Heavenly Avarice,
   That never could be satisfied,
That did incessantly a Paradice   10
Unknown suggest, and som thing undescried
     Discern, and bear me to it; be
     Thy Name for ever praisd by me.

2
     Parched my Witherd Bones
And Eys did seem: My Soul was full of Groans: 15
     My Thoughts Extensions were:
Like Steps and Paces they did still appear:
     They somwhat hotly did persue,
     Knew that they had not all their due;
     Nor ever quiet were: 20
But made my flesh like Hungry Thirsty Ground,
   My Heart a deep profound Abyss,
And evry Joy and Pleasure but a Wound,
So long as I my Blessedness did miss.
     O Happiness! A Famine burns,   25
     And all my Life to Anguish turns!

3
     Where are the Silent Streams,
The Living Waters, and the Glorious Beams,
     The Sweet Reviving Bowers,
The Shady Groves, the Sweet and Curious Flowers,   30
     The Springs and Trees, the Heavenly Days,
     The Flowry Meads, the Glorious Rayes,
     The Gold and Silver Towers?
Alass, all these are poor and Empty Things,

undescried, unseen, undiscerned, unexplored

35   Trees Waters Days and Shining Beams
        Fruits, Flowers, Bowers, Shady Groves and Springs,
        No Joy will yeeld, no more then Silent Streams.
            These are but Dead Material Toys,
            And cannot make my Heavenly Joys.

                        4

40   O Love! ye Amities,
        And Friendships, that appear abov the Skies!
            Ye Feasts, and Living Pleasures!
        Ye Senses, Honors, and Imperial Treasures!
            Ye Bridal Joys! Ye High Delights;
45   That satisfy all Appetites!
                Ye Sweet Affections, and
        Ye high Respects! What ever Joys there be
            In Triumphs, Whatsoever stand
        In Amicable Sweet Societie
50   Whatever Pleasures are at his right Hand
            Ye must, before I am Divine,
            In full Proprietie be mine.

                        5

        This Soaring Sacred Thirst,
        Ambassador of Bliss, approached first,
55   Making a Place in me,
        That made me apt to Prize, and Taste, and See,
            For not the Objects, but the Sence
            Of Things, doth Bliss to Souls dispence,
                And make it Lord like Thee.
60   Sence, feeling, Taste, Complacency and Sight,
            These are the true and real Joys,
        The Living Flowing Inward Melting, Bright
        And Heavenly Pleasures; all the rest are Toys:
            All which are founded in Desire,
65   As Light in Flame, and Heat in fire.

Proprietie, property, possessions; *Complacency*, tranquil pleasure, contentment

From the Burney Manuscript

The Return

To Infancy, O Lord, again I com,
   That I my Manhood may improv:
   My early Tutor is the Womb;
      I still my Cradle lov.
   'Tis strange that I should Wisest be,   5
   When least I could an Error see.

Till I gain strength against Temptation, I
   Perceiv it safest to abide
   An Infant still; and therfore fly   10
      (A lowly State may hide
   A man from Danger) to the Womb,
   That I may yet New-born becom.

My God, thy Bounty then did ravish me!   15
   Before I learned to be poor,
   I always did thy Riches see,
      And thankfully adore:
   Thy Glory and thy Goodness were
   My sweet Companions all the Year.   20

Shadows in the Water

In unexperienc'd Infancy
Many a sweet Mistake doth ly:
Mistake tho false, intending tru;
A *Seeming* somwhat more than *View*;
   That doth instruct the Mind   5
   In Things that ly behind,
And many Secrets to us show
Which afterwards we com to know.

Thus did I by the Water's brink
Another World beneath me think;
And while the lofty spacious Skies
Reversed there abus'd mine Eys,
      I fancy'd other Feet
      Came mine to touch and meet;
As by som Puddle I did play
Another World within it lay.

Beneath the Water Peeple drown'd.
Yet with another Hev'n crown'd,
In spacious Regions seem'd to go
Freely moving to and fro:
      In bright and open Space
      I saw their very face;
Eys, Hands, and Feet they had like mine;
Another Sun did with them shine.

'Twas strange that Peeple there should walk,
And yet I could not hear them talk:
That throu a little watry Chink,
Which one dry Ox or Horse might drink,
      We other Worlds should see,
      Yet not admitted be;
And other Confines there behold
Of Light and Darkness, Heat and Cold.

I call'd them oft, but call'd in vain;
No Speeches we could entertain:
Yet did I there expect to find
Som other World, to pleas my Mind.
      I plainly saw by these
      A new *Antipodes*,
Whom, tho they were so plainly seen,
A Film kept off that stood between.

abus'd, deceived; *Antipodes*, place diametrically opposite as Australasia is from
Europe on the globe

By walking Men's reversed Feet
I chanc'd another World to meet;
Tho it did not to View exceed
A Phantasm, 'tis a World indeed,
  Where Skies beneath us shine,   45
  And Earth by Art divine
Another face presents below,
Where Peeple's feet against Ours go.

Within the Regions of the Air,
Compass'd about with Hev'ns fair,   50
Great Tracts of Land there may be found
Enricht with Fields and fertil Ground;
  Where many num'rous Hosts,
  In those far distant Coasts,
For other great and glorious Ends,   55
Inhabit, my yet unknown Friends.

O ye that stand upon the Brink,
Whom I so near me, throu the Chink,
With Wonder see: What Faces there,
Whose Feet, whose Bodies, do ye wear?   60
  I my Companions see
  In You, another Me.
They seemed Others, but are We;
Our second Selvs those Shadows be.

Look how far off those lower Skies   65
Extend themselvs! scarce with mine Eys
I can them reach. O ye my Friends,
What *Secret* borders on those Ends?
  Are lofty Hevens hurl'd
  'Bout your inferior World?   70
Are ye the Representatives
Of other Peopl's distant Lives?

Of all the Play-mates which I knew
That here I do the Image view
75   In other Selvs; what can it mean?
But that below the purling Stream
          Som unknown Joys there be
          Laid up in Store for me;
To which I shall, when that thin Skin
Is broken, be admitted in.

On Leaping Over the Moon

I saw new Worlds beneath the Water ly,
    New Peeple; and another Sky,
        And Sun, which seen by Day
        Might things more clear display.
5   Just such another
            Of late my Brother
Did in his Travel see, and saw by Night
    A much more strange and wondrous Sight:
Nor could the World exhibit such another,
10   So Great a Sight, but in a Brother.

Adventure strange! No such in Story we
    New or old, tru or feigned, see.
        On Earth he seem'd to mov
        Yet Heven went abov;
15   Up in the Skies
            His Body flies
In open, visible, yet Magick, sort:
    As he along the Way did sport
Like Icarus over the Flood he soars
20   Without the help of Wings or Oars.

Line 3: 'And' changed from 'Another'. Traherne's original line probably read
'another Sun by Day/Did things more clear display'.
Lines 19–20 have been returned to the original. Philip wrote: 'Over the Flood he
takes his nimble course/Without the help of feigned Horse.'

As he went tripping o'r the King's high-way,
    A little pearly River lay
       O'r which, without a Wing
       Or Oar, he dar'd to swim,
          Swim throu the Air   25
          On Body fair;
    He would not use nor trust *Icarian* Wings
    Lest they should prov deceitful things;
For had he faln, it had been wondrous high,
    Not from, but from abov, the Sky: 30

He might hav dropt throu that thin Element
    Into a fathomless Descent;
       Unto the nether Sky
       That did beneath him ly,
          And there might tell   35
          What Wonders dwell
On Earth abov. Yet bold he briskly runs
    And soon the Danger overcoms;
Who, as he leapt, with Joy related soon
    How *happy* he o'r-leapt the Moon.   40

What wondrous things upon the Earth are don
    Beneath, and yet abov, the Sun?
       Deeds all appear again
       In higher Spheres; remain
          In Clouds as yet: 45
          But there they get
Another Light, and in another way
    Themselvs to us *abov* display.
The Skies themselvs this earthly Globe surround;
    W'are even here within them found.   50

Lines 37–38 as first written. Philip wrote: 'Yet doth he briskly run,/And bold the
Danger overcom.'

On hev'nly Ground within the Skies we walk,
  And in this middle Center talk:
    Did we but wisely mov,
    On Earth in Hev'n abov,
55   We then should be
        Exalted high
Abov the Sky: from whence whoever falls,
  Through a long dismall Precipice,
Sinks to the deep Abyss where *Satan* crawls
60   Where horrid Death and Despair lies.

As much as others thought themselvs to ly
  Beneath the Moon, so much more high
    Himself he thought to fly
    Above the starry Sky,
65   As *that* he spy'd
        Below the Tide.
Thus did he yield me in the shady Night
  A wondrous and instructiv Light,
Which taught me that under our Feet there is
70   As o'r our Heads, a Place of Bliss.

To the same purpos; he, not long before...

To the same purpos; he, not long before
  Brought home from Nurse, going to the door
    To do som little thing
    He must not do within,
5   With Wonder cries,
        As in the Skies
He saw the Moon, O *yonder is the Moon*
  Newly com after me to Town,
  That shin'd at Lugwardin but yesternight,
10   *Where I enjoy'd the self-same Light.*

purpos, purpose; *Line 2,* note 'going' changed from 'went'

As if it had ev'n twenty thousand faces,
  It shines at once in many places;
    To all the Earth so wide
    God doth the Stars divide
      With so much Art   15
      The Moon impart,
They serve us all; serv wholy ev'ry One
  As if they served him alone.
While evry single Person hath such Store,
  'Tis want of Sense that makes us poor.   20

From the *Thanksgivings*

Thanksgivings for the Soul

I will sing of the mercies of the Lord for ever: with my mouth will
I make known thy faithfulness to all Generations.

    And the Heavens shall praise thy Wonders O Lord: thy
faithfulness also in the Congregation of the Saints.

    The Heavens shall praise thy Wonders: 5
      But more the Powers of my immortal Soul.

    Which thou hast made more excellent than the Clouds, and
greater than the Heavens!

    O Lord I rejoyce, and am exceeding glad;
        Because of thy Goodness,   10

In { Creating the World.
       Giving Brightness to the Sun.
       Ruling the Sea.
       Framing the Limbs and Members of my Body.

    But much more abundantly,   15
      For the Glory of my Soul:

Lines 1–4, from Psalm 89.1, 5

Which out of Nothing thou hast builded,
　　To be a Temple unto God.
A living Temple of thine Omnipresence.
20　　　An understanding Eye.
A Temple of Eternity.
　　A Temple of thy Wisdom, Blessedness, and Glory.
　O ye Powers of mine immortal Soul, bless ye the Lord, praise
him, and magnifie him for ever.
25 He hath made you greater,
　　More glorious,　　Brighter,
　　　Better than the Heavens.
A meeter dwelling place for his eternal Godhead
　　Than the Heaven of Heavens.
30 The Heaven of Heavens,
　　And all the Spaces above the Heavens,
　　Are not able to contain him.
Being but dead and silent Place,
　　They feel not themselves.
35 They know nothing.
　　　See no immensity nor wideness at all.
But in thee, my Soul, there is a perceptive Power

$$\left. \text{To} \begin{cases} \text{Comprehend the Heavens.} \\ \text{Feel thy self.} \\ \text{Measure all the Spaces beyond the Heavens.} \\ \text{Receive the Deity of the eternal God,} \end{cases} \right.$$

40

　　　And those Spaces,
　　　　By him into thee.
To feel and see the Heaven of Heavens,
45　　All things contained in them,
　　　And his Presence in thee.
Nor canst thou only feel his Omnipresence in thee,
　　But adore his Goodness,
　　　Dread his Power,
50　　　Reverence his Majesty,
　　　See his Wisdom,

Lines 23–24, from the *Benedicite*

Rejoyce in his Bounty,
Conceive his Eternity,
Praise his Glory.
Which being things transcendent unto place,   55
Cannot by the Heavens at all be apprehended.
  With Reverence, O God, and Dread mixed with Joy, I come
before thee.
  To consider thy Glory in the perfection of my Soul,
    The Workmanship of the Lord,   60
      In so great a Creature.
From $\begin{cases} \text{East to West} \\ \text{Earth to Heaven,} \end{cases}$
    In the twinkling of an eye
      My Sight removeth,   65
Throughout all the Spaces beyond the Heavens:
My Thoughts in an instant like the holy Angels.
  Nor Bounds nor Limits doth my Soul discern,
    But an infinite Liberty beyond the World.
Mine Understanding being present   70
    With whatsoever it knoweth.
  An infinite Bulk excludeth all things.
    Being void of Life, is next to nothing.
      Feeleth not it self,
      Is a dead Material,   75
      Vain, Useless. But
I admire, O Lord, thine infinite Wisdom; $\left\{\begin{array}{l} \textit{O give me} \\ \textit{Grace to} \\ \textit{understand} \\ \textit{its Excellency.} \end{array}\right.$
  In advancing me to the similitude
    Of thine eternal Greatness.
  A Greatness like thine   80
    Hast thou given unto me.
  A living Greatness:
    A Soul within:
    That receiveth all things.

A Greatness $\left\{\begin{array}{l} \text{Spiritual.} \\ \text{Heavenly.} \\ \text{Divine.} \\ \text{Intelligent.} \\ \text{Profitable.} \end{array}\right.$ $\begin{array}{l} \textit{That doth not fill,} \\ \textit{but feeleth all} \\ \textit{Things. Receiveth,} \\ \textit{seeth, discerneth,} \\ \textit{enjoyeth them.} \end{array}$ 85

90   Blessed be the Lord,
        Whose Understanding is infinite,
      For giving me a Soul
        Able to comprehend with all Saints the length, and breadth,
and depth, and heighth of the Love of God, which passeth
95 Knowledge, that I might be filled with all the fullness of God.

      Unsatiable is my Soul,
        Because nothing can fill it.
    A living Centre, wider than the Heavens.
175   An infinite Abyss,
    So made by the perfection of thy Presence,
      Who art an infinite *KNOWLEDGE* in ev'ry Centre;
      Not corporeal, but simple Life;
      Wonderfully sufficient in all its Powers,

180   Objects   { Material,
                           { Immaterial.
    For all {   / Earthly,
                            | Heavenly,
            Operations { Temporal,
185   \ Eternal;
      A work worthy of Immortality!
  To create an endless unsensible Body,
      Is not the way to Celestial Greatness.
  A Body endless, though endued with Sense,
190   Can see
        Only visible things,
    Taste
        The Qualities in Meat and Drink,
    Feel
195   Gross or tangible Bodies,
    Hear
        The harshness or melody of Sounds,
    Smell

Lines 93–95, from Ephesians 3.18–19; *unsensible*, not of the senses, not able to be perceived by the senses

The things that have Odours in them.
But those things which neither Sight, nor Smell, nor Taste, 200
can discern, nor Feeling try, nor Ear apprehend,
The Cream and Crown and Flower of all,

Thoughts,	Counsels,
Kingdoms,	Ages,
Angels,	Cherubims,

205

The Souls of Men,

Wisdom,	Holiness,
Dominion,	Soveraignty,
Honour,	Glory,
Goodness,	Blessedness,

210

Heroick Love,
yea
GOD HIMSELF,
Come not within the sphere of Sense:
Are all Nullities to such a Creature. 215
Only Souls, immortal Souls, are denied nothing.

How infinite is thy Thirst,
That we should perform the thing thou desirest!
O Lord!
Thou so loved'st us, 460
That for our perfect Glory,
Thou didst adventure into our hands
A Power of displeasing thee.
Which very confidence of thine ought more to oblige me,
than all the things in Heaven and Earth, faithfully to love thee. 465
But wo is me, I have sinned against thee.
I have sinned, O Lord,
And put an Object before thee
Which thou infinitely hatest.
An ugly Object, 470
Of infinite Deformity;
From which it is impossible
Thou should'st turn away thine eyes.
And hadst thou not loved me

With a greater Love
475   Than all this,
I must, like *Lucifer*,
          Have sunk into the Pit
              Of eternal Perdition.
But thou hast redeemed me.
480   And therefore with Hallelujahs
          Do I praise thy Name.
Recounting the ancient Glories
      Which thou createdst in my Soul:
          And confessing,
485   That infinitely more is left unsaid.
          O my God,
              Sanctify me by thy Spirit.
              Make me a Temple of the Holy Ghost,
              A willing Person in the day of thy Power.
490   Let my Saviour's Incarnation be my Exaltation;
      His Death, my Life, Liberty, and Glory;
          His Love, my Strength,
              And the incentive of mine;
          His Resurrection, my Release;
495   His Ascension, my Triumph;
          His Gospel, my Joy;
          The Light of his Countenance,
              (And of thine in him)

500   My $\left\{\begin{array}{l}\text{Reviving,}\\\text{Healing,}\\\text{Comforting}\end{array}\right\}$ Sun.

In the day of thy Grace, let me work for thy Glory;
          Rejoyce in thy Goodness;
And according to the wideness of mine Understanding,
505   The Greatness of my Soul,
          The Liberty of my Thoughts,
              Walk at large
      In all the Regions of $\left\{\begin{array}{l}\text{Heaven and Earth,}\\\text{Time and Eternity;}\end{array}\right.$
510   Living in thine Image

Towards all thy Creatures;
On Angels wings,
Holy Meditations.
According the transcendent Presence of my Spirit everywhere,   515
Let me see thy Beauties,
Thy Love to me,
To all thy Creatures.

In the { First Creation,
Government of Ages,   520
Day of Judgment,
Work of Redemption,

In { My Conception and Nativity,
All my Deliverances,
The Peace of my Country,   525
Noah's Ark.

With *Moses* and *David*,
Let me behold thy ways,
Delight in thy Mercies,
Be praising thee.   530
O shew me the excellency of all thy works!
In the Eternity that is before the World began, let me behold
the beauty of thine everlasting Counsels.
And in the Eternity which appeareth when the World is ended
let me see thy Glory.   535

*O God of infinite Majesty, now I confess that the Knowledge I have of thee
is admirable, by that which I discover in my self: for if in a thing so gross as
is my Body, there be a Spirit so noble as is my Soul, which giveth it Being
and Life, governeth it, and in it and by it worketh such stupendious things;
how much more necessary is it that thou be in the midst of this extended*   540
*World, who art that supream Spirit, by whom we all are, live, move, and
have our being. Since therefore thou art my Being and my Life, thou art my
Soul too, and I rejoice to have thee for my God, loving thee infinitely more
than my self. O that all did know thee, and love thee more than their Life
and their own Soul, since thou art the true Life and Soul of all: To whom*   545
be Glory, Honour, and Praise, for evermore. Amen.

From *The Ceremonial Law*

Moses Face

Instructed after forty days he came
Untoucht, & safe from out the burning flame.
That Cloud did yeeld Substantial Tables, and
He brought them down in Stone with in his Hand.
5   That Darksom Myste that seemd so great a Night,
Made him Illustrious, by its Greater Light.
Twas his Mount Tabor, for transfigurd there
His face did like the Burning Sun appear.
Beams darted from it twenty thousand Ways,
10   His Brow like Golden Hornes extended Rays.
Rays dissipate the Gloomy pich that shrouds
Him round about, he breaks out from the Clouds
More bright ten thousand fold: When Aaron came
With joy to meet him, seeing a Man of flame
15   Approach, he fled; & all his friends did flie
His presence, as a Dreadfull Prodigie
At first: His Eys & Eylids were so pure
His Cheeks & forhead they could not endure,
To shew that Moses Angelick flesh shall be
20   As Bright & full of Immortality
As Glorious vigorous & strong as theirs, nay his
Whose Dying Body purchasd all this Bliss.
We cannot long be conversant with Light
That is Divine, Eternal, Infinite,
25   And ever Blessed; but we shall become glorious
Like Myrrors formd into the Sun.
And when the Light of Gods own Countenance
Is seald on ours, as we our pace advance
To Mortalls that were left behind, we are
30   Their Terror first, at last their Joy & Care.

The Light we bring amazes them awhile,
At last the Terror turns into a Smile.
The Danger & the Dread being Safe & Sweet,
As ever tis when Joys & Terror meet.
From Contemplations & Devotions he   35
Returning seemd a lesser Deitie
And as the Sun breaks from a Cloud more fair
And gilds the late Storm suffering purged Air
With Stronger beams, so Saints from Martyrdom
Or from Distress, or Persecution come.   40
Affliction lind with Contemplation is
A Cloud disguising a full Mount of Bliss.
But Moses knew not that his face did Shine,
He that is humble he is most Divine.
Who sees not his own Brightness; yet he does giv   45
A Lustre shewing where his Spirit lives
And when hes made to see it vails his Face
Concealing those Perfections that do grace
His Soul within; & when he needs must feel
The Strength & Glory doth adoring Kneel.   50
Yet Willingly as twere unwittingly imparts
Inflaming Bright Informing Healing Darts,
And all his Light & Love Communicates
Freely to all that mov with in his Gates.
For then in truth we only are divine,   55
When Wisdom Love & Goodness in us shine,
And being full of Heavenly Blessedness
Ourselvs, make others with us to possess
The Glory we enjoy: or gently strive
At least their putrid Coarses to revive   60
And fill their Tents with that Diviner Light
Which in the Mountain ravished our Sight.

The Inside

When God had spoken to the ruder Crowd,
His 10 Comandments or Words aloud,
The people trembled at what they admired,
And not being able to endure, desired
Moses, for fear of Death, to interpose,
And for themselvs a safer Distance chose.
Frail flesh & Blood's not able to endure
His neer approach, he is so great & pure.
Men promise to themselves Som great Delight,
Could they but once enjoy the Glorious Sight
Of God on Earth, . . .

Here *The Ceremonial Law* ends unfinished.

Selections from *Christian Ethicks*

In *Christian Ethicks*, Traherne's extensive work on Christian virtues, gratitude is the final virtue. Final in its place at the end of the work, and final because it is the culmination of the other virtues. And so I have chosen this extract from the first of his three final chapters on gratitude. Much of Traherne's social ethic is gratitude in action; we must not only give thanks but do thanks. Gratitude is an expression of the soul that has wanted and been filled, the soul engaged in the dynamic of gift and receipt that marks the meeting of human need and divine plenitude. Traherne calls gratitude a virtue 'mixt of satisfaction and praise' and it may be that gratitude is offered as a counterbalance to his elsewhere rampant insatiability.

Christian Ethicks, mainly a prose work, also contains a few poems. The first of the two represented here, 'Contentment is a sleepy thing', suggests the importance of desire to felicity. The second poem, 'For Man to Act', also found in *The Kingdom of God*, helped to identify the Lambeth Manuscript as Traherne's.

From Chapter XXXII

Of Gratitude. It feeds upon Benefits, and is in height and fervour answerable to their Greatness. The Question stated, Whether we are able to love GOD more than our selves. It is impossible to be grateful to GOD without it. A hint of the glorious Consequences of so doing.

There is ever upon us some pressing want in this World, and will be till we are infinitely satisfied with varieties and degrees of

Glory. Of that which we feel at present we are sensible: when that want is satisfied and removed, another appeareth, of which before we were not aware. Till we are satisfied we are so clamorous and greedy, as if there were no pleasure but in receiving all: When we have it we are so full, that we know not what to do with it, we are in danger of bursting, till we can communicate all to some fit and amiable Recipient, and more delight in the Communication than we did in the Reception. This is the foundation of real Gratitude, and the bottom of all that Goodness which is seated in the bent and inclination of Nature. It is a Principle so strong, that Fire does not burn with more certain violence, than Nature study to use all, when it hath gotten it, and to improve its *Treasures* to the acquisition of its *Glory*. . . .

TO talk of overflowing in the disbursments and effusions of Love and Goodness, till our emptiness and capacity be full within, is as impertinent and unseasonable, as to advise a Beggar to give away a Kingdom, or a dead man to breathe, or one that is starving to give Wine and Banquets to the Poor and Needy. But when a man is full of blessedness and glory, nothing is so easie as to overflow unto others: to forbid, or hinder him, is to stifle and destroy him. Breath with the same necessity must be let out, as it is taken in. A man dies as certainly by the confinement, as the want of it. To shut it up and deny it are in effect the same. When a man hath the glory of all Worlds, he is willing to impart the delights wherewith he is surrounded, to give away himself to some amiable Object, to beautifie his Life, and dedicate it to the use and enjoyment of Spectators, and to put life into all his Treasures by their Communication. To love, and admire, and adore, and praise, in such a case are not only pleasant, but natural, and free, and inevitable operations. It is then his supream and only joy to be amiable and delightful. For the actions of Love and Honour belong in a peculiar manner to a plentiful estate: Wants and Necessities when they pinch, and grind us in a low condition, disturb all those easie and delicate Resentments, which find their element in the midst of Pleasures and Superfluities. . . .

THAT we are to *Enjoy* all Angels and Men by communicating our selves unto them, is a little *mysterious*: but may more easily be

understood, than a thing so obscure as *The Enjoyment of GOD by* 40
way of Gratitude. That we are to love GOD more than our selves
is apparently sure, at least we ought to do it, but whether it be
possible, is a question of importance. That we gain infinitely by
his Love, is certain; but that we gain more by our own, is prodigious! It is our duty to love him more than our selves, but whether 45
it be our Nature, or no, is doubtful. It is impossible to ascend at
the first step to the top of the Ladder. Even *Jacobs* Ladder will
not bring us to Heaven, unless we begin at the bottom. Self-love
is the first round, and they that remove it, had as good take away
all: For he that has no love for himself can never be obliged. 50
He that cannot be obliged cannot delight in GOD: He that cannot delight in him cannot enjoy him: He that cannot enjoy him,
cannot love him: He that cannot love him cannot take pleasure
in him, nor be Grateful to him. Self-love is so far from being
the impediment, that it is the cause of our Gratitude, and the 55
only principle that gives us power to do what we ought. For the
more we love our selves, the more we love those that are our
Benefactors. It is a great mistake in that arrogant *Leviathan*, so far
to imprison our love to our selves, as to make it inconsistent
with Charity towards others. It is easie to manifest, that it is 60
impossible to love our selves, without loving other things:
Nature is crippled (or if it has her feet, has her head cut off) if
Self-preservation be made her only concern: We desire to live
that we may do something else; without doing which life would
be a burden. There are other principles of Ambition, Appetite, 65
and Avarice in the Soul: And there are Honours, and Pleasures,
and Riches in the World. These are the end of Self-preservation.
And it is impossible for us to love our selves without loving
these. Without loving these we cannot desire them, without
desiring cannot enjoy them. We are carried to them with greater 70
ardour and desire by the love of our selves. Preservation is the
first, but the weakest and the low'st principle in nature. We feel it
first, and must preserve our selves, that we may continue to enjoy
other things: but at the bottom it is the love of other things that
is the ground of this principle of Self-preservation. And if you 75

Leviathan, Thomas Hobbes' 1651 book that laid the foundation for Western political
philosophy's social contract theory

75   divide the last from the first, it is the poorest Principle in the
World. . . .
I make it a great Question, would men sink into the depth of
the business, Whether all Self-love be not founded on the love
of other things? And whether it be not utterly impossible
80   without it? Only the love of those things is so near and close
to the love of our selves, that we cannot distinguish them, but
mistake them for one and the same. If the Sun were
extinguished, and all the World turned into a Chaos; I suppose
there are few that love themselves so, but they would die, which
85   plainly shews that the love of the World is inseparably annexed
with the love of our selves, and if the one were gone, the other
would be extinguished: especially if the sweetness of the Air,
and its freedom and ease, were changed into fire and torment.
For then we would surely desire to die, rather than endure it:
90   which shews that the love of ease and repose is greater than the
love of our very Beings, though not so perceivable, till we have
examined the business. But if there be any pleasure, or
goodness, or beauty truly infinite, we are apt to cleave unto it
with adhæsion so firm, that we forget our selves, and are taken
95   up only with the sence and contemplation, of it. The
ravishment is so great, that we are turned all into extasie,
transportation and desire, and live intirely to the object of our
fruition. The power of infinite delight and sweetness is as
irresistible, as it is ineffable. And if GOD be all beauty and
100 delight, all amiable and lovely, truly infinite in goodness and
bounty, when we see him, and taste the grace of his excellency,
the blessedness and glory wherewith we are amazed, possesseth
us intirely and becometh our sole and adæquate concern. After
that sight it is better perish and be annihilated, than live and be
105 bereaved of it. The fall from so great a height would fill the
Soul with a cruel remembrance, and the want of its former
glory and bliss be an infinite torment. Now if it loved nothing
but it self, it could endure all this; rather than forsake it self, or
lose, or be bereaved of its essence, it would endure any misery
110 whatsoever. Or to speak more correct and accurate sence, it
would be incapable of any Passion, Patience or Misery, but only

that which flow'd from its abolition. Nothing could prejudice it but the change of its Being....

WERE there no SUN it were impossible for so fair an *Idea* to be conceived in a Mirror, as is sometimes in a Glass, when it is exposed to the skie. The Mirror is in it self a dark piece of Glass; and how so much fire, and flame, and splendor should come from it while it is a cold Flint or piece of Steel, how it should be advanced by any Art whatsoever to so much beauty and glory, as to have a Sun within it self, and to dart out such bright and celestial beams no man could devise. Yet now there is a Sun, the Matter is easie, 'tis but to apply it to the face of the Sun, and the Glass is transformed. And if GOD dwelleth in the Soul as the Sun in a Mirror, while it looketh upon him, the love of GOD must needs issue from that Soul, for *GOD is love*, and his love is in it. The impression of all his Beauty swallows up the Being of the Soul, and changes it wholly into another nature. The Eye is far more sensible of the Day, and of the beauty of the Universe, than it is of it self, and is more affected with that light it beholds, than with its own essence. Even so the Soul when it sees GOD is sensible only of the glory of that eternal Object: All it sees is GOD, it is unmindful of it self. It infinitely feels him, but forgets it self in the Rapture of its Pleasure.

BUT we leave Illustrations, and come to the reason of the thing in particular. The Soul loving it self is naturally concerned in its own happiness, and readily confesseth it oweth as much love to any Benefactour, as its bounty deserveth. And if the value of the Benefit be the true reason of the esteem, and Reason it self the ground of the return, A little Kindness deserveth a little love, and much deserveth more. Reason it self is adapted to the measure of the good it receiveth, and for a shilling-worth of Service, a shilling-worth of Gratitude is naturally paid. For a Crown or a Kingdom the Soul is enflamed with a degree of affection that is not usual. Now GOD created and gave me my self; for my Soul and my Body therefore I owe him as much as my Soul and Body are worth: and at the first dash am to love him as much as my self.

Idea, form, pattern; *is sensible of*, is cognizant of, aware of

Heaven and Earth being the gifts of his love superadded to the former, I am to Love him upon that account as much more as the World is worth; and so much more than I love my self. If he hath
150   given all Angels and Men to my fruition, every one of these is as great as my self, and for every one of those I am to love him as much as that Angel or Man is worth. But he has given me his Eternity, his Almighty Power, his Omnipresence, his Wisdom, his Goodness, his Blessedness, his Glory. Where am I? Am I not lost
155   and swallow'd up as a Centre in all these Abysses? While I love him as much as all these are worth, to which my Reason, which is the essence of my Soul, does naturally carry me, I love him infinitely more than my self; unless perhaps the possibility of enjoying all these things makes me more to esteem my self, and
160   increases my Self-love for their sake more than for my own. Thus when I see my self infinitely beloved, I conceive a Gratitude as infinite in me, as all its Causes. Self-preservation is made so natural and close a Principle, by all the hopes and possibilities to which I am created. Those Hopes and Possibilities are my tender concern:
165   and I live for the sake of my infinite Blessedness. Now that is GOD: And for his sake it is that I love my self, and for the glory and joy of delighting in him, I desire my continuance; and the more I delight in him, my Continuance is so much the more dear and precious to my self. Thus is GOD infinitely preferred by
170   Nature above my self, and my Love to my self, being thoroughly satisfied, turns into the Love of GOD, and dies like a grain of Corn in the Earth to spring up in a new and better form, more glorious and honourable, more great and verdant, more fair and delightful: more free, and generous, and noble; more grateful and
175   perfect. The Love of GOD is the sole and immediate Principle upon which I am to act in all my Operations. . . .

BY his Love he existeth eternally for our Enjoyment, as the Father of GLORY which is begotten by it self: but we do not gain all this by his Love; but by our own. Some man would say, We gain
180   our Souls and Bodies by the Love of GOD, all Ages and Kingdoms, Heaven and Earth, Angels and Men, infinite and eternal Joyes, because all these were without our care or power prepared by him, and his love alone. They were prepared indeed

by *his* Love, but are not acquired, or enjoyed by it. *He so loved the World that he gave his only begotten Son*, and with him all the Laws and Beauties of his Kingdom: but unless we love him, unless we are sensible of his Love in all these, and esteem it, we do not enjoy our Souls or Bodies, Angels or Men, Heaven or Earth, Jesus Christ or his Kingdom: Rather we trample upon all, and despise all, and make our selves deformed. All these do but serve to increase our Damnation, and aggravate our Guilt, unless we love and delight in their Author, and his Love it self will eternally confound us. So that we gain and enjoy the Love of GOD by ours. Now Love returned for Love is the Soul of Gratitude. In that act, and by it alone, we gain all that is excellent: And beside all these become illustrious Creatures. . . .

NOW to love GOD is to desire Him and his Glory, to esteem him and his Essence, to long for him and his Appearance, to be pleased with him in all his Qualities and Dispositions, or (more properly) in all his Attributes and Perfections, to delight in all his Thoughts and Waies. It is to love him in all his Excellencies. And he that is not resolved to love every Excellency in him, as much as it deserveth, does not love GOD at all: for he has no design to please him. But he that purposes to do it, must of necessity love GOD more than himself, because he finds more Objects for his Love in GOD, than in himself; GOD being infinitely more excellent than he. But if this seem a grievous task, it is not a matter of *Severity*, but *Kindness*. We mistake its nature, the Duty does not spring from any disorder in GOD, not from any unreasonable or arrogant *Selfishness*, as base and foolish men are apt to imagine, but from his Excellency: it *naturally* springeth from the greatness of his *Worth*: And it is our *freedom*, when we see his infinite Beauty, to love it as it *deserveth*. When we so do, we shall infinitely love it *more* than our selves: because it is infinitely *better*. And indeed, shall find it so conveniently seated in the Deity for us, that could it be transposed or remov'd, it would no where else be fit for our fruition. It is that eternal act of Love and Goodness that made all the Kingdom of Glory for us: that Care and Providence that governs all Worlds for our Perfection, that infinite and eternal Act that gave us our Being. That Beauty is it self the Deity, and wherever it appeareth there GOD is. The GOD-HEAD is the Beauty in which we are all made perfect. And because we *were* nothing, we must be infinitely pleased that he *is* eternal; because it is his eternal Act that gives us a Being: and the Act, Oh how 225 Divine! It is his Beauty and Glory. Can we chuse but love that Act, which is all Goodness and Bounty! Which prepares for, and gives to, us, infinite felicity! If we love our selves we must needs love it, for we cannot forbear to love the fountain of all our delights, and the more we love it, the more ardently we delight in 230 it, the sweeter and more transporting will all our Raptures be, the more feeling and lively, the more divine and perfect will our Souls and our Joyes be: When we know GOD, we cannot but love him more than our selves: and when we do so, his Blessedness and Glory will be more than ours; we shall be more than Deified, 235 because in him we shall find all our Perfection, and be eternally Crowned. We must of necessity sit in his Throne, when we see him enjoying all his Glory, because his Glory is his Goodness to us, and his Blessedness our Felicity: Because in the acts of our Understanding we shall eternally be with him, and infinitely be 240 satisfied in all his Fruitions. That Excellency which obliges us, will enable us to love him more than our selves: and while we delight in him for our own sakes, we shall steal insensibly into a more divine and deeper Delight, we shall love him for his. And even in point of Gratitude adore his Glory.

245   TO *Adore* and *Maligne* are opposite things: to *Envy* and *Adore* are inconsistent. Self-love is apt to leap at all advantages, and the more we love our selves, the more prone we are to covet and wish whatsoever we see Great and Excellent in another. But he hath conquered our Envy by his infinite Bounty: and made us *able* to 250 adore him by the Perfection of his Essence. To covet the Perfections of him we adore, is impossible. It is impossible to adore him whom we would spoil, and rob of his Perfections. For Adoration is a joyful acknowledgment of the infinite Perfections of an *Adorable* Object, resting sweetly in them with acquiescence 255 and rejoycing. It is prone to add and to offer more. An adoring Soul is in the act of sacrificing it self to the Deity, and with infinite Complacency admiring and adoring all his Glories.

HIS Glories will be inspired into the Soul it self, for the healing of that Envy to which it is otherwise addicted. And instead of Robbery, and Discontentment, and Blasphemy, and Covetousness, the Soul shall be full of Honour and Gratitude, and Complacency: and be glad to see its GOD the full and eternal act of Perfection and Beauty. It was from all eternity impossible there should be any other but he; and he from all eternity has so infinitely obliged us, that were it possible for any other to have been, it would not be desirable. He hath obliged us, and we love him better than any other. Should we fancy or conceive another, a Power from all Eternity acting, should we suppose it possible that a Power besides him might have bin; it must be just such a Power as this is, and act just in such a manner as this hath done: or it would be displeasing. This hath done all that we can desire, all that all Powers infinite and eternal can do *well*; and therefore all possible Powers are conceived in him. He is the full and adæquate object of all Desire; because the Fountain of all the most Glorious things, and the sole perfect cause of all Enjoyment whatsoever. 260 265 270 275

Complacency, contentment, tranquil pleasure

'Contentment is a sleepy thing' from Chapter XXXVII 'Of Contentment'

Contentment is a sleepy thing!
If it in Death alone must die;
A quiet Mind is worse than Poverty!
Unless it from Enjoyment spring!
5   That's Blessedness alone that makes a King!
Wherein the Joyes and Treasures are so great,
They all the powers of the Soul employ,
   And fill it with a Work compleat,
      While it doth all enjoy.
10   True Joyes alone Contentment do inspire,
Enrich Content, and make our Courage higher.
      Content alone's a dead and silent Stone:
         The real life of Bliss
      Is Glory reigning in a Throne,
15   Where all Enjoyment is.
The Soul of Man is so inclin'd to see,
Without his Treasures no man's Soul can be,
      Nor rest content Uncrown'd!
         Desire and Love
20   Must in the height of all their Rapture move,
      Where there is true Felicity.
Employment is the very life and ground
Of Life it self; whose pleasant Motion is
         The form of Bliss:
25   All Blessedness a life with Glory Crown'd.
Life! Life is all: in its most full extent
Stretcht out to all things, and with all Content!

'For Man to Act as if his Soul did see' from Chapter XXI 'Of Courage'

For Man to Act as if his Soul did see
The very Brightness of Eternity;
For Man to Act as if his Love did burn
Above the Spheres, even while its in its *Urne*;
For Man to Act even in the Wilderness,   5
As if he did those Sovereign Joys possess,
Which do at once confirm, stir up, enflame,
And perfect Angels; having not the same!
It doth increase the Value of his Deeds,
In this a Man a Seraphim exceeds: 10
    To Act on Obligations yet unknown,
To Act upon Rewards as yet unshewn,
To keep Commands whose Beauty's yet unseen,
To cherish and retain a Zeal between
Sleeping and Waking; shews a constant care;   15
And that a deeper Love, a Love so Rare,
That no Eye Service may with it compare.
    The Angels, who are faithful while they view
His Glory, know not what themselves would do,
Were they in our Estate! A Dimmer Light   20
Perhaps would make them erre as well as We;
And in the Coldness of a darker Night,
Forgetful and Lukewarm Themselves might be.
Our very Rust shall cover us with Gold,
Our Dust shall sprinkle while their Eyes behold   25
The Glory Springing from a feeble State,
Where meer Belief doth, if not conquer Fate,
Surmount, and pass what it doth Antedate.

Line 25, *sprinkle* could mean 'sparkle' in the sixteenth–seventeenth centuries; *Antedate*, anticipate

Selections from the *Select Meditations* and *Commentaries of Heaven*

Select Meditations

The *Select Meditations* are a collection of meditations arranged, like the *Centuries*, in groups of 100. Probably written when Traherne was in his twenties, they are at once more public and more private than much of his other work. In their intermingling of public and private concerns we may see a young Traherne exploring his vocation in a time in which Christian ministry was inseparable from the making of political choices. The self-scrutiny of his Puritan education, still fresh in his mind, surfaces in his many confessions and in the enumeration of faults that not only give *Select Meditations* its distinctive emphasis on sin, less evident elsewhere in his works, but also some fresh insights into Traherne's character.

I.93

A Broken and a contrite Heart is made up of knowledge Sorrow and Lov: knowledge of our primitiv felicitie in Eden, Sorrow for our fall, Lov to God so Gratious and Redeeming. know ledg of our Happiness in being Redeemed, Sorrow for sin
5 against our Redeemer, Lov to God yet Continuing favorable and Gracious. knowledg of the Joys prepared for us, Sorrow for our unworthyness in living beneath them, Lov to God for his Goodness Magnified and Exalted over us. one Broken Sigh, or Contrite Groan is more Acceptable to God, then Thousands of
10 Rams, and ten Thousand Rivers of oyl, and maketh more pleasant musick in his Eares, then all the fained musick of the Spheres. Which because it is so He Botleth up our Tears. for they Abide in

the places wherever because they are pearls, Dissolved pearl, Tho
not vanishing; which he reserveth in Store for the Holy Angels.
Neither is this Metaphorical, He really Bottleth all our Teares. For   15
they Abide in the places where they fall, and in those Moments
wherei[n] they were Shed, are Treasured up for all Beholders. are
not all the parts of all Eternitie present at once to God; are not all
their contents present in them, Is not all Eternity present [to] our
understanding: if not in us! How then shall it otherwise be, but   20
that Gods Eternitie is a Bottle like the Heavens Wherein the Tears
of Penitents Glitter like the Stars; Scattered at a Distance, yet all
before us! O my God since I know my selfe the Joy of Angels in
Repenting, the very knowledge of that Shall encreas my Tears,
Sweeten my Sorrow, Alleviat yet Augment and compleat my   25
Repentance. Were it not for the Sun no vapors would arise, Light
immitted rarifies and prepares them. Light Emitted makes them
Transpire. Light Refl[e]cted Elivates in Counion. Light immitted,
Emitted, and reflected as they all ascend refines and carries them.
without Light there would be no vapors; without which vapors   30
recondensing into clouds, there would be no Rain, no fruits, no
flowers. clouds of Penitence ma[y] seem to overwhelme and
oppress the Face, but not appear till first raised by the Sun of
Righteousness Shining on the Earth which is Mans Heart. Light
immitted is Glory Seen, which melts and Soften[s], Light Emitted   35
is Lov returned, which Transpires as Sighs and bears us upwards,
light reflected is the means of Grace Shining [on] the Soul, and
cooperating with the Spirit, which works within us With Sighs
and Groans unutterable. without which sighs There can be no
clouds Tears fruits or flowers. Since Therefore Repentance is a   40
work of the Light, and Sin can never be Hated but in the open
day, since those clouds on the face of Happienes Beautifie the
Heavens, fructifie the Earth, and make it flourish, Since the world
is the better for some Rainy Days, and Sinners Tears are Dissolved
pearl that Shine for-ever, I will not be without some o[f] those,   45
but Esteeme Repentance Disguised Happieness. And wonder at
God for making every Thing a part of Eternal Blessedness.

I.94

Eternity is a Sphere into which we Enter, all whose parts are at
once Standing round a bout us. How else could all its parts before,
and after, be objects present to the understanding. Eternitie in the
Dark is an Object upon the Earth, Therefore Seems an Empty
5   Space prepared before us. But is with God an Eternal Day, whose
Evening and morning and noon are present: and in every part also
the Things with which they are filled. Eternitie that was before the
creation may seem the Morning wherin all Things began [t]o Bud
and flourish, Eternity after the world is Ended may seem the
10 evening, wherein all are at Rest in Heavenly Peace and receiv the
fruits of their Labors. Eternity now as it Surrounds the world, may
Seem the Noon and Heat of the Day, wherin all things are growing
and creatures labouring: but indeed all These are at once in God,
changeable in them selves and succeeding each other, but standing
15 there and A-biding for ever. Otherwise the Eternity before the
world would be indeed the Evening, for the evening and the
morning were the first Day, or the Empty Darknes and Space of
time wherein God was without the Emanations of his Goodness in
the works of his Hands, and Things were not. The Eternity of the
20 world, the womb of the Morning in which it began, All Things
then having their Birth and spring: The Eternity which is to
Endure when Time is Done, the High Noon of Meridian Glory.
But Oh wonderfull is the Eternal God who is Himselfe his own
Eternity! How Glorious is the world which wheather it be the
25 Morning or noon of His kingdom we cannot tell! How Happy are
we that Liv in a world so Glorious, where Eternity is on every Side
a Standing Object of Divine Enjoyments for evermore!

I.95

So wonderfull is the Incomprehensibility of the Divine Essence,
that the world was with God from all Eternity. It was not, and yet
was. It was not in it selfe, for it had a Begining Some 5000 years
agoe: yet was in God. for he being his own Eternity, must of
5   Necessity include it. for out of Eternity nothing can be nor can any
Thing at all begin to be within it. Begin in it selfe every Thing may,
and must except God. But the very moment in which every Thing

Begins is included in Eternity, and Tho other moments were a
Great while before it, and many Succeed it, it is a Standing object,
which can never possibly remove from Its place. Tis we are   10
Successiv, Eternity is not so. Trees in a walk are past by, Tho them
Selves stand still. And to him that runs seem to run Backward. The
moments Stand, we mov by, and cry the Time passeth away. As we
go forward the time passeth and seems to go behind us: But cannot
move or Stir. what infinite liberty is there in His Kingdom!   15

II.34

O my God how infinite art thou in Goodness! How I in
unworthyness! I loath and abhor my Selfe; who have Sinned
a[gainst] the Light of thy countenance! The works of Darkness
have Blinded mine Eys. And Since my Baptisme, and Since my
Repentance I have Greiveously Sinned. Insomuch that all the   5
creatures in Heaven and Earth may rise up against me. Especialy
thy Saints may justly Abhor me! I admire O Lord the exceeding
Multitude of thy Tender Mercies. that thou sufferes[t] me to
flourish in any of their affections, that I am not cast, as an
Abominable Branch out of the Kingdome. O my God I Greive   10
and am ashamed that I must make such a Confession. but my
Guilt is Great, blot it I beseech Thee out of the Book of thy
Remembrance. And wheras I have Deserved utter Darkness, O let
my Soul be Humbled within me, and thine Infinite Mercies be
exalted over me. Spare me O Lord and b[e] Reconciled to me,   15
and my Love Shall be more Enflamed unto Thee! O Let the Sun
of Righteousness arise upon me! O Let hi[s] Bloud Sprinkle me!
Let the Holy Ghost O Lord overshadow me, that I may conceive
of Thee Such Glorious Things, as may be worthy of thy
Blessedness and Eternal Majesty, and the Grea[t] joy of thy   20
Church and people. O let a Sinners Lips out of the Depth of Hell
praise Thee. Guilt is Hell. and the Blindness wherby a Sinner is
Divided from Thee, a Mist Like the Blackness of Eternal
Darkness! O Let this confession stan[d] here as a Token How I
loath and abhor my selfe! I have deserved to be vile in mine own   25
eys, And I abhor my Selfe in Dust and Ashes. But Thou O Lord
remember a contrite and broken Heart, and How Thou hast

promised to Dwell within it. Let this Blot which appeareth a-
mong my joyes, Shew thy mercy and their Beauty more! O
30   manifest thy Selfe, and Dwell within me! Giv me care to Sin no
more! By sin I am Divided from Thee my God, and onely by thy
Grace can be restored againe to the Light of thy Countenance.
Nor can I ever Shew forth the Glory of thy Lov, but in the Light
of thy presence, where all the fullness of joy appeareth! O Lord
35   my God I rejo[y]ce in Thee!

II.35

O my God How am I to Admire and Adore Thee forever more,
that am called to live in the similitude of thy Blessedness and in thy
Blessedness. Thou hast So obliged me in makeing me Like Thee,
that Thy Blessednes is more then mine, becaus my Blessed[nessl is
5   made Like thine. For as Thou art, so am I forevermore. The Light
of thy Kingdom, the Joy of thy Saints, a Temple of thy Glory, and
the End of all Things. O my God I Tremble at my Ignorance! And
acknowledg my selfe a prodigie by reason of my sin. Shall I be as
Gall and Shame, to them before whose faces I ought to be a King
10   Amiable in Holiness Joy and Glory. O let me never sin more! never
be Remiss, never careless! if the Displeasure of my freind be such
Greife unto me, O what is thine if it is not, O what will it! I
beseech Thee keep me, O keep me that I may Sin no more!

II.36

As a prisoner returning from the pitt, as a Malefactor Saved
from the cross, yea as a Devill taken out of Hell, I return O Lord
to the Glory of thy kingdom. For my crime hath been wors then
Satans. Having Sinned more, O more, much more in Sinning
5   against my ReDeemers Lov! How Sweet then will the Glory be
to which I am restored, and How Delightfull his Lov, by whom I
was Redeemed. O prince of peace who sittest at the Right Hand
of God in the Glory of the father I Adore Thee. and Desire to Dye
for Thee, or to Liv to please Thee. Thy Lov, O thy Lov is Better
10   then Heaven! It is indeed the very only Sun and Soul of Heaven.

prodigie, a wonderful example of some quality

II.40

But after all to be Beloved is the Greatest Happieness. All This
Glory and all these Treasures, being but the Appendencies, and the
ornaments of that person that is our Bride or Freind, prepared all
for the Sake of Lov, to commend and Sweeten it more unto us.
But How Great must His Lov be, who not onely created the   5
Heavens and the earth for one, but becaus a Lover is the sweetest
thing, and Himselfe the most Glorious Lover, created the most
Glorious Image of Himselfe to giv us and made many Millions of
Angels Cherubims and Men to Honor and Attend that Image,
that Like a God He might be Lov unto us! Nay How Glorious   10
and full of Wisdom is that work, that maketh every one of Those
Attendants So Glorious a Sovereign that being after his Similitude
the supreme of all, He Should Still be an Attendant to that Single
Image who was our First Freind, and yet Himselfe the principal
Lover and all the Residue His Attendants! every one being So the   15
Sun in Heaven among the plannets! Yet is all this Atcheived by
Lov, for God is Lov. And all this shews his Lov unto my Soul. Yea
it Shews indeed that for which I intirely Lov Him, that He is
Infinite Lov to every Soul!

II.42

Blessed be the Eternal God for shewing me the Treasures of
Felicity! O what could this world be, but a silent chaos, a Dull and
Empty wilderness, were [it] not for the Invisible Things of His
Eternal Kingdom! When all other Comforts fail, when the Sword
hath wasted our land, when our Cittys are Destroyd, when our   5
Assemblies are Fled, when nothing is near but woefull
Solitariness, the Soul that can Liv in Communion with Him shall
Sing His praises: And be to it selfe a Temple of Delights, and
Assemblies and Treasures! yet will the Face of His Happieness be
Disguised, with Lamentations for his people: Silent venerations of   10
Gods Justice that hath made him naked, an Awfull Dread of his
High Majestie and Great Judgments which have so latly
happened, will be his food.

Appendencies, appendages

II.66

Those that think our union with God so Incredible, are taught
more in the Sacrament. He gives Himselfe to be our food. is
united to us. Incorporated in us. for what doth he intimate by the
Bread and wine, but as the Bread and wine are mingled with our
5 flesh, and is nourishment Diffused through all our members, So
he is Lov mingling with our Lov as flame with flame, Knowledge
shining in our knowledge as Light with Light, An omnipresent
Sphere within our Sphere.

II.67

There be many things wherein the modestie of Man is an
Injurious Counterfeit. Not modestie, but Ignorance, Ingratitude
and Thraldom, for such is that that is afrayd to acknowledge the
Benefits of God; and unwilling to perceiv the Good it hath
5 received. Had I said that the Son of man while we Sit Down will
Gird Himselfe and come forth to Serv us; I should hav been
accused by men to hav Spoken Blasphemie. But now he hath said
it, it is Beleived: but Hastily, past over, and not understood. yea
many read that never take Notice He spake any Such Thing.
10 Blessed are those Servants whom the Lord when he commeth
shall find watching: verylie I say unto [you] that He Shall Gird
Himselfe and make them Sit down to meat, and will come forth
and serve them. what kind of service will Jesus doe? Shall the king
of Glory come and Gird Himselfe and come and Serve Such
15 Abjects as we, who dare presume to think thus Arrogantly of
Himselfe! O Man Consider, what Service wouldst thou have him
to do! Were He like thy Servant at thine own Disposal what
wouldst thou require? wouldst thou have him come and wash thy
feet? He hath washed them with His Bloud! wouldst thou have
20 Him reach thee New wine in the kingdome of Heaven, while
thou Sittest at the table! He will do it! not in cups but in whole
Hogsheads Seas and Oceans. Alas! couldst thou ever have
Contrived Such a Service, either So profitable to Thee or So vile
to Him, as His comming Down from Heaven to Dye for Thee!

Hogsheads, large casks or measures for liquid

He doth Greater Things for Thee, then Thou darest presume to 25
Ask. What Greater Condescention, then that the king of Glory
should leave His fathers Throne, and be basely mangled Upon a
Crosse for thy Sin! He is wont to do Greater Things then Man
dare beleive. And now He is Ascended, Doth He Gird Himselfe as
thy Servant (to whom Angels Minister) to Governe all Things and 30
to prepare thy Joys in making them fit to be enjoyed. In the
kingdom of Heaven Thou Shalt Sit at the Table; when Thou art
awakened to Consider these Things.

II.71

That God should give us soe Divine a Power! To Transfigure all
Things, and be Delighted!

II.72

Shadows in the water are Like their Substances. And So reall, that
no Painter can againe Express them. even here beneath the sun is
seen, and the face of Heaven. O give me more of that Spirit, wherby
we strongly Lov and Delight each in other. whereby we Liv in each
other[s] soul, and feel our Joys and sorrows! The Father is crowned 5
in God the Son, The Eternal Son in God the father. And both
obeyed in obedience to the Holy Ghost. one will in three persons.
But are they not one in Essence too! one in Felicity, one in Lov! All
Treasures are the fathers in the Son, All Joys are the sons in the Holy
Ghost. The Holy Ghost is the Lov of the father and the Son 10
Dwelling in us, or to speak plainly seene by us. For as the sun when
it shines on a Mirror, is seen within it: So Love when it is seen,
Ravisheth the Soul becaus it toucheth it, and Dwelleth in the
understanding by which it is seen, and the sight of it Enflameth the
soul with Lov againe. the Lov seen is the Lov returned. or else 15
Exchangeth, Dwelling there and Begetting its Similitude. Three
Persons united in Lov, are one in Essence: or what ever Difficulty is
in that word, one by the Best of all possible unions.

III.27

Till custom and Education had bred the Difference: it was as
obvious to me to see all within us, as It was without. As easy and as

natural to be Infinitly wide on the Inside, and to see all Kingdoms Times and persons within my Soul, as it is now to see them in the
5 open world. Nay verily it was more natural, for there was a comprehensiv Spirit, before ther was an Eye. And my Soul being Like him, did first expect to find all things in it Selfe, before it learned to See them without it. It would be a Great wonder if God Should See any thing out of himSelfe. And but that he hath made
10 the world would be still wonderfull. Were nothing made but a Naked Soul, it would see nothing out of it Selfe. For Infinit space would be seen within it. And being all sight it would feel it selfe as it were running Parrallel with it. And that truly in an Endless manner, becaus it could not be conscious of any Limits: nor feel it
15 Selfe Present in one Centre more then another. This is an Infinit Sweet Mystery: to them that have Tasted it. For before I had Bodily Journeys I was immediately Present in any kingdome, and Saw the people in it, Trees Ground and Skies in as strong a Light, as ever I saw the Kingdom where I am. I scarsly Dream'd of any outward
20 way that Led unto it. And did as vigorously feel them to be my Treasures Delights Enlargments as ever I did feel any Money mine or Tree or Gardens or meadows since.

No Tongue can tell what Treasure are in Store
What Joyes shall Dwell in those that him Adore.
25 Mens souls unless they better measure keep,
Are most a wake when most they seem to sleep.
When most they seem to wake are most a sleep.

For when they are awake, they see Things with their Bodily Eys: but their souls sleep, becaus they see not with their understandings.
30 If their souls are Drownd and hav Lost their Liberty, they Dream and are asleep wakeing. being therefore asleep, they think those who Liv by their soul to be onely Dreaming. How is it possible that all the Things in the whole Hemisphere should be represented in a Looking-glass, and that all the Things in Heaven and Earth
35 should not in a Soul, which is a more Glorious Mirror. Seest thou not How vigorously and realy thy face is seen in a Glass, bring it out to the open Heavens, and the Heavens shall be as truly represented in it. The sun shall shine as strongly in it as it doth in the skies, O the Reality! O the Room! O the lenght and Breadth

and Depth that is in the molten steel! And shall not all Things more   40
realy Individualy and truly be seen Abiding in the Hous and
Temple of Almighty God! O man, thy Soul is capable of an Eternal
Day, far more then a Mirror is of the Earth and skies!

III.30

When I come from the Scholes, haveing there heard them
dispute De Ente, De forma materiali, D[e] Quid-ditate, and Such
like Drie and Empty Theames: when I came from the Heathen
Poets, Having seen their vanities Dreames and fables: or else from
the market haveing there seen a great deal of chaffering about cloth   5
and Money, and things more Drie then Haecceities and fables. Yea
when I come from Taverns haveing there seen Roaring Boys, that
can swear and swagger and wallow in their vomitt: O what a
Glorious thing is that Kingdom which in the Temple I behold!
How doth it overflow with Living waters to Refresh a Droughty   10
Soul. whence ever I come I find it. Amiable and Sweet. my only
and resting Place. seas of Amber, or far more Rich, Mountains of
Gold, or far Better, Territories more Kingly, then Angels else can
tell How to frame. Laws sweeter then the Hony comb, souls and
mansions more wide then the Heavens, such Heavens as Adam   15
Saw, affections Better then Sun Beams, yet Sun Beams Better then
Rivers of melted Pearl, Golden Thrones and crowns of Love, and
all these endlessly multiplied in all Ages. O the joy, the food, the
Satisfaction! where ever else I am, being a Stranger unto these I am
a Husk with Swine. not a Prodigal but a very Husk a-mong them.   20
A Husk in respect of Emptines. A Prodigal in respect of want, nor
ever am I Happy till I return Home.

III.43

God is Goodness infinitly Communicativ. God is Lov – infinitly
Delighted to see us Happy. God is Wisdom and Delighteth to giv
us all His Treasures, in the wisest manner. God is Almighty, and
loveth to Satisfie his Infinit Goodness, and Delight His Lov, and

---

Haecceities, qualities that make a thing describable as 'this', particular characteristics,
individualities

5   shew wisdom, in makeing our Happieness compleat and Exquisite.
Being all these he Delighteth in the utmost Exaltation and Glory.
Doing theref[or] for us the Best of all possible Things, to satisfie his
Nature He would make His Image, concerning which Image the
Divines and scholmen hav apprehended too short, and spoken
10   superficialy. They tread over a living River to the other side, and
Leav all that which should reviv the Grass and cherish the Trees and
make the Shore to flourish behind them. Bounty follows the
Nature of God, as Light doth the sun, or a shadow its Body. Being
therefore infinitly Bountifull He is infinitly willing to Give all
15   Things. And that He may so do in the most perfect manner, creates
His IMAGE to giv it unto. which Image they tell us consisteth in
Righteousness and true Holyness, but for want of Drinking that
River I Spoke of, Diminish the Beauty and Glory of the Shore by
arriving at it to suddainly. They are silent in this, that man is made
20   after Gods Image in respect of Ability capacity and power. And
because I never had the Happieness of seeing this, I knew not the
Glory of the Divine Image. Nor the Beauty of Holiness, nor the
Excellent nature of that Righteousness unto which it was made.
nor did I see the reason of Gods wayes, nor the Greatness of his
25   Lov. Being Infinit in Bounty, and willing to make His Image, He
made a creature Like Him to behold all Ages, And to Love the
Goodness of evry Being in all Eternity, and of every Excellence in
evry Being. That by Seeing, it might receive, and enjoy by Loving,
all the Things in Heaven and Earth. And be as God Himselfe who
30   enjoyeth all by Seeing and by Loveing them. His works being made
thus the Image of God in Similitude of power, and Infinitly
Beloved, God desireth His freind or Son Should use these Powers.
Apply his mind to the Beauty of all His wayes, and render all
Things a Due Esteem, Loveing the Goodness which therein is
35   Seated. By Doing this I become Righteous and Holy, the Image of
God in Exercises most Blessed and Glorious, His Admired Idea,
among men and Angels. The Sole Possessor of all His Treasures,
most pleasing unto Him in all the works of Happieness and Beauty.
For the perfect complacency they take in me Reigning in the
40   Bosom of all spectators. For then are we Righteous when we
render to all a Due esteem. And then Holy when we do thus with

such Infinit Zeal, That we would not for worlds miscarry in a Tittle. Being more Glorious as we are our Selves workers, then as we are our Selves Receivers of all things. God desiring to accomplish His work, not onely in Giving, but in makeing us to receive in the most perfect Manner. which is so to receiv that we may be Glorious in Receiving as He in Giving. more Glorious in Returning then we are in Receiving, more Happy as Suns, then Temples, more Happy as Sons, then Suns, but most Happy in being Brides and Freinds.

III.46

The Divine Image consisteth more in Doing then Enjoying, in Shining then Receiving; in being then in haveing all Treasure. By this we are, what by the other we are Intended, And Imitate God in Blessing and Giving. we receive all Treasures for this End, that we may be a Treasure. A Treasure unto God, a Treasure unto Angels, a Treasure unto men: an Infinite Treasure Deep and Exquisite, in the full enjoyment of Infinit Treasures. And Highly Beautifull in all their Eys by Imitating God of our own Accord. How wonderfully am I bound to magnifie his Name, that I am a Treasure to Such Infinit Treasures. How Rich is the world, wherin I have Such possessions. How Glorious is God who is a father in a family of such children. How Beautifull are those works which He Infinitly Desireth. How Joyfull am I and how Blessed a-mong all my Treasures. How odious is a Sin after such obligations. How Beautifull and Glorious is Gods kingdom. How Dreadfull and miserable is mans Blindness. How much are Souls to be thirsted, How Strait is the way of returning Home!

III.65

Profound Inspection, Reservation and Silence; are my Desires. O that I could attain them: Too much openness and proneness to Speak are my Diseas. Too easy and complying a Nature. Speaking too much and too Long in the Best Things. Mans nature is Nauseating and weary. Redundanc is Apprehended even in those Things of which there can be never Enough. by Exposing Himselfe a man Looseth Him Selfe, and becometh cheap and common. The vices of men have made those Things vices, that are

the Perfections of Heaven. There Shall we Sing His Praises all the
Day Long. With David my Soul Shall make her Boast in the Lord.
Here it [is] Tediousness and vain Glory. There it is the Joy of all
to be Communicativ and He most Happy that is Infinitly So. Here
He is unwelcom. The Ignorance of man maketh those Things
obscure that are Infinitly Easy, those things ugly that are in them
selves Beautifull, those Things inconvenient that are in them selves
Blessed. Here I am censured for Speaking in the Singular number,
and Saying I. All these Things are done for me. Felicity is a Bird
of Paradice So Strang, that it is Impossible to flie a mong men
without Loseing some feathers were She not Immortal. There it
shall be our Glory and the Joy of all to Acknowledge, I. I am the
Lords, and He is mine. Every one shall Speak in the first Person,
and it shall be Gods Glory that He is the Joy of all. Can the freind
of GOD, and the Heir of all Things in Heaven and Earth forbear
to say, I. we must attend the Reverence Due unto our Persons. And
so far yeeld to the corruptions of men, as to strengthen our
Influence in Bringing them to Glory. Their Incapacity hath made
that saying Eminent and necessary. Silere Tibi, Laus est. There we
Shall have one open and Eternal Day, here our Lives must be
Intermingled as time is in this world, with Speech and Silence,
Dayes and nights. There our Glory shall be Exposed unto all. Here
it cannot be understood. There it Shall be seen: but God Almightye
most Highly Remembred. It is Inconvenient here to [be] Exposed
unto many. Bright Be and Humble: that is Divine and Heavenly
on the Inside.

III.66

Temperance in Expression is the Art a mong the Sons of Men.
They suspect a Depth, and see Majesty in few words. We have
millions of Things to utter and Declare which are Infinitly clear
and Rich in them selves But must utter them by Drops; becaus
they seem Dull and Dubious. O the misery of confined Man!

III.67

As my work of calling others is Greater then to Enjoy, So ought
my Care in that work. O my God who Lovest the manner better

Silere Tibi, Laus est, it is praiseworthy in you to be silent

then the Deed, Delineat in my Soul an Exquisite Ability, that I
may Express it in my Life with Exquisit care.

III.78

Mans Humility and Gods Highness are wedded objects to each
other. Let me see the Nothing out of which I was taken and I
Shall See the Glory to which I am exalted. Thy Glory and my
Lowness increas and perfect my Happiness. of both which while
I am Sencible I Sencibly feel my Eternal Fulness. For as the 5
Heavens a bove are in a Mirror seen, as far beneath them, as they
are a bove, and both Conjoyned make an Intire Sphere, Seeming
Divers but the very Same; So doth God and my nothing, both
Apprehended. For while I see both I am infinitly Greater. An
infinit Distance is between God and the Highest cherubim: an 10
infinite Distance between Nothing and the Lowest Sand. Nothing
Less then an infinit power being able out of Nothing to creat a
Sand. while I contemplat the nothing out of which I was made,
in the Bottom of my being I See his Glory. And at once possess
the Zenith and the Nadir of his Eternal Sphere, the Heights and 15
Depths of His Infinit fullness. And by How much the Lower the
valley is out of which I am raised, by so much the Higher the joy
is to which I am exalted. God at the Bottom being the same God,
with Him that Reigneth in the Highest Throne. And my
Happiness Greater to all Eternity, by how much the Less from 20
Eternity it was. yea from all Eternity far Greater then if I had been
from Everlasting. God and I are more Blessed in what whatsoever
is. I more obliged to Lov his Goodness for makeing me out of
Nothing: and He more Exalted, while I obliged. He more pleased
by How much the more I am Delighted, and I more Blessed, 25
while He is Pleased. From all Eternity to my First Conception I
was Nothing, from my first Conception to all Eternity I am a
being. From all Eternity my Being was with God Almighty. to all
Eternity my Nothing will be before my Face. From all Eternity to
all Eternity my nothing and my Being Endless and unmovable: 30
and I in both infinitly Greater, the Joy of Angels and Men both
infinitly Greater. that being Best which forever is. God seen all
Activity Life and Power, in raising me from nothing to infinit

Glory. Humility is the Bride and Queen of God: The Lowest
35 foundation and the Highest Throne: The Earth removed and the
Heavens seen: Gods fulness in Mans Emptiness Best Appearing.

III.79

He that will be Happie must see his wants that He might See
his Treasures for his Treasures. For as pictures are made by a
pleasant Admixture of Lights and shades so is Happines
compleated by a fulness and variety of wants and Treasures. wants
5 and Enjoyments go hand in hand. They infinitly agree while they
seem to differ. For without want there Could be no Enjoyments,
but all Redundancies and Superfluities, for which respect even
want it selfe is a soveraign possession. From all Eternity God
wanted us, or else we could not be Superadded to him. From all
10 Eternity God included us, and therefore He could not at all want
us, we Could not at all be Superadded to Him. we could not be
superadded to him, could we not be made His Treasures, we could
not be superadded to Him becaus we were in Him. From
everlasting He was before us, from Everlasting He was within us,
15 from everlasting He was beyond us, with us and without us, from
everlasting Infinitly present, near and Distant, His Goodness
wanted us and that is His Glory. It is the Glory of God that he
loves to be Enjoyed. Who Loving to be enjoyd we are the
Treasures of his Goodness, becaus its Recipients. Blessednes
20 Naturaly Loveth to be seen, and is Like milk in a womans Breasts
more Delightfull in being Distributed, then in Lying Still in its
own Fountaine. It curdleth there and recoyling upon it selfe: in
flowing from the mother it feedeth a nother and becometh
usefull. Delightfull to the mother while it is usefull. But this in
25 God is Incomprehensible. For as Fountaines are Flowing all into
the Sea, at the Same time they are derived from them: and are all
Extant, and surrounded at once within the Heavens, Soe all these
Emanations of Delight are extant in God and at once enjoyed.
From everlasting we wanted on[e] to give us a Beginning and
30 Therefore is God an Infinit Treasure, because He supplieth that
necessity. Had all Things been from everlasting in them selves
there had been neither place nor occation for Gods Goodness.

Had all things been from everlasting in Him, from everlasting we might all behold his Glory. And soe we shall. For becaus it is necessary to see our wants, before we can See and Possess our Treasures, our wants and Treasures Shall be forever present, casting a sweet Reflection upon each other, that we might Equally be Effected, and with both Delighted. But O the Abysses of Endless Eternity! O the Riches and Depths that are in it! Where even wants them selves Glitter in a fulness of Eternal Treasures. And are all present, tho all supplied, that they might the more be seen!

III.82

God is a Fulness in all Extremes: Happieness a mistery in which contrarieties are coincident: And Glory an Abysse in which contradictions unite, and reconcile them selves. He is an Infinit Sphere, yet an infinit Centre. He is infinitly before us yet infinitly after us. we are Equal to Him, yet infinitly beneath Him. And more Blessed then if we had been from Everlasting. By obliging us to Lov Him more then our selves He hath [made] us Blessed as Himselfe is. By makeing us Blessed as Himselfe is He hath made us infinitly beneath Him. By makeing us each a Possessor of Eternity and the End of all Things He hath made us Like Himselfe. By makeing us Like Him hath exalted us to his Throne and by doing so made us his Peers. All like Him, of whom it is said, Arise O sword and smite the man that is my Fellow. No Distance was convenient between God and us, but that of obligation. We are infinitly beneath Him, becaus infinitly obliged.

III.83

When I see a Little church Environed with Trees, how many Things are there which mine Eye discerneth not. The Labor of them which in Ancient Ages Builded it; the conversion of a Kingdom to God from Paganism, its Protection by Laws, its subjection to Kings, its Relation to Bishops, usefulness and convenience for the Entertainment of christians, The Divine Service, office of the ministery, Solemn Assemblies Prayses and Thanksgivings, for the sake of which it was permitted, is Governed, Standeth and Flourisheth. Perhaps when I Look upon

10   it, it is Desolate and Empty almost Like an heap of Stones: non of
these things appearing to the Eye, which nevertheless are the
Spirituall Beauties which adorn and clothe it. The uses Relations
services and Ends being the Spiritual and Invisible Things: that
make any material to be of worth. He that cannot see Invisible
15   cannot Enjoy nor valu Temples. But He that Seeth them may
Esteem them all to be his own: and wonder at the Divine Bounty
for giving them so Richly becaus were there non such, and he
able to Erect them, for these End[s] it were very Amiable that
Himselfe should Endow them. The Services are such that He
20   should Delight in; and becaus so rejoyce in God for Preparing
them to his Hands. Especialy I who have been nourished at
universities in Beautifull Streets and famous colledges, and am
sent thither From God Almighty the maker of Heaven and Earth,
to teach Immortal Souls the way to Heaven, to sanctifie his
25   Sabbaths, to instruct them in his Laws Given upon mount Sinay,
and to shew them the Lov of a Glorious Saviour Slain upon
mount Calvary: to Lead them by his Merits to Eternal Joys.

Commentaries of Heaven

Commentaries of Heaven was an enormously ambitious work that
Traherne never completed. This collection of prose and verse
'commentaries', or explorations on a range of themes, was to be
a mammoth encyclopaedia, a practical 'A' to 'Z' of theology.
Traherne began with 'Abhorrence' and, nearly 400 pages of neat,
compact writing later had only got as far as 'Bastard'. How much
longer the work would have grown before Traherne reached 'Z'
can only be imagined. Some of the 94 'commentaries' are
systematic studies, some collections of thoughts, most of them end
with a poem. What I have given here are snippets from much
more extended considerations on two topics: 'Spiritual Absence'
and 'Affections'.

From 'Spiritual Absence' (folios 8r–9v)

Nothing can be more against nature, either in GOD, or MAN, than to giv Abilities without Objects. That we hav Abilities therfore is a Sure foundation of infinit Hope: for nothing can be more contrary to Divine Wisdom, or Goodness, than to implant such, as we hav received, & to leave them Desolate without Enjoyment. If they hav no Objects, they are seated in us to no purpose; & being lively, would Torment us. Which evidently shews it against our Nature. Yet for all this, we are bereaved of the Benefits, designed by their Union, through a Careless Ignorance that divides us from them, by dividing our Abilities from all their Objects . . .

Two of the effects of Spiritual Absence:
Wickedness:

> Because being Absent from our Treasures our strength is gone, we hav lost all Sence of Divine Alluremts, Encouragements, Obligations; which ought to fix us. So that we are quickly shaken with any Temptation. He that Seeth an infinit Treasure is unwilling to leav it for a farthing: but he that Dreams not of it, can forsake it for nothing.

Covetousness:

> The Soul is naturaly infintly Covetous, & fitly so. When therfore it hath lost the tru Treasures, it most Greedily followeth the Treasure of Darkness.

Under the heading 'The Desolatness of Absence':

> To satisfy these Powers and Inclinations, being Absent from GOD, is to feed upon Delusions. Yet he is Desolat, that cannot satisfy them. Inferior, fickle unworthy Objects, are

Dust & Ashes always, often Dreams & somtimes Thorns. To
shun the Miserie of Being Desolat, among them, is to be
like a King Divested of his Ornaments, jesting with
Beggars. But in GODS presence all our Powers &
inclinations are Satisfied. He Sees us, Seeks us, Lovs us
infintly, Tenders us as His Ey, Esteemeth our Persons,
Prizeth our Lov, advanceth us to His Throne, Delighteth in
our Wisdom, Crowneth our Courage, giveth us Objects of
Admiration & Pleasure, is always with us, surroundeth us
with Kingdoms Ages & Eternity taketh Pleasure in our
Affection, & in so Stupendious a Maner Magnifies us, that
He does all Things for us, & delights in all the Felicites of
his Kingdom for our Sakes. Can any endure to be Absent
from Him?

Spiritual Absence

Is not the Greatest Death that ere can be,
A Seperation from Felicitie?
And what is Absence, had we but the Sence
To feel its Sad and Direfull Consequence?
5   If GOD the Glory be of Souls, their Life
And Lov: then Seperation is the Knife
That kills a Soul! And we the Pain of Sence
Should feel, but that we're slain. An Influence
Doth truly from the Pain of Loss arise
10   Begetting Pain of Sence in him that Dies.
But Miseries are not perceivd, while Men
In Syrens Laps do lie, or Satans Den.
He that is Dead alive, when He doth die,
Shall Quickend be to feel his Miserie.
15   And present be with Him forever more
To whom in Life He Absent was before.

Quickend, brought to life, revived

From 'Affection' (folios 48r–54r)

Affection

The Number, Nature & Extent of the Affections, their Use & End, their Original & their Objects are here to be considered, where we speak of Affection in the General before we come to their Particular Kinds as these of Anger Lov &c we shall reserve many Mysteries that will more properly be opened in the Affections of fear & Hope, Love & Desire, Sorrow Joy &c. in their proper places. Their order & Degree; & the several maner of their Existence in their various Subjects is here to be observed to which we may adde also their Diseases, & their Cures.

Its Nature

Affection, if we respect the Etymologie of the Word, is plain enough; This endangerd rather to be obscured by a Description, then to need one, Evry one Knowing that to Affect, is to produce some Kind of Qualitie, or Sence, or Inclination, Some new Effect or other, in the Thing Affected; tho Sometimes it is taken (& here especialy) for some New Passion produced in the Soul Affecting. I am not Ignorant that to Affect, & be affected are Identical Termes, being shut up & involved in one Another: for evry Affection includeth Some thing of Action & Passion together. Anger is Stiled an Affection of the Soul, & so is Sorrow, & Love & Joy & Fear because upon the Sence of such an Object, the Soul is affected in such a Maner. Tis Affected with some new Action of Liking or dislike in relation to that Object. Which as it is impressed by that Object is a Passion; as it is an Operation exerted by the Soul it is an Action. And this Action as long as it continues, tho it be a transient Thing, & a meer Motion of the Mind seems a permanent & setled Quality, because the soul is clothed in it, as if it were an Habit, from which it differs only in Duration.

Its Effects

Our Affections meet either with Sensible Objects, or Insensible. Insensible Objects may be Affected by us in one sence, but not in another. We may affect them so far as to change our selvs; but cannot produce any change in them by our meer Affection because we cannot affect them with a Sence of what we feel and doe. But Objects endued with understanding are capable of being affected by us both ways. We can love them & move them to love, rejoyce in them & cause them to rejoyce, be angry with them, & make them angry, griev because of them, & cause them to griev; fear them, desire them, hope for them, flie from them, persue them, despair of them, &c. And many times our Affections alone which change us work many changes in them, one living Object affecting another Activly & passively at the same time. The sight of their Beauty produceth Love in us, & the sence of our love produceth Hope Love Joy & desire in them. And thus it may be said of all the Affections.

The Effects of them in our selvs are so strong, that sometimes they end in Death Sickness, poverty Labor, Extasie, Emprisonment Famine, Shame and Glory. These being all produced by our Affections, together with our greatest Happiness or Misery. The Effects of them in others are so important, that our Affections are the greatest Causes of Contentmt or disturbance unto them. And by a long distant Propagation, the Beauty Order Peace & Prosperity of the world, or the Confusion of it, ariseth from the interior Motion of Humane Affections. Nay sometimes one mans Affection alone is the Health or Destruction of a whole Nation. All Amity, Unity, Delight & Pleasure proceeding from Affection, as all their Contraries do in like Maner. For which caus Affections may seem the fountains of Weal or Woe, And Kind & Good Affections those Streams of living Water; that satisfy refresh & comfort, the thirsty & weary soul of Man. These naked Principles may be heigh[t]ned to the utmost Degrees of Violence.

[Here Traherne lists at length their kinds in general.]

A Correllarie
From this Observation of the Afections & their kinds in general, we may lawfully conclude that men may learn how to shew their Affections. It being their Duty to make their Affections of the most excellent Kind. For since any Affection is capable of being

Humane, Bruitish or Divine, we that aspire naturaly to perfection, ought so to form the Motions of our Soul, as to make our Sorrow, Love, Joy, Desire, Anger, Hope & fear all Divine, because Divinity is the Perfection of Humanity, as its Crown and End. But of this we are to speak more in the Cure of their Diesease. Any Affection in General may be made Bruitish Humane or Divine. Temporal or Eternal, Permanent or Transeunt.

Affection

1

Affections are the Wings and nimble feet
The Tongues by which we taste whats Good and Sweet.
The Armes by which a Spirit doth embrace,
Or thrust away; the Spurs which mend its Pace.
As Apprehensions are pure Sparks of Light   5
Hands to lay hold on things, Ideas bright
Thoughts Sences or Intelligences, Things
Being seen in spirit; or reverst the stings
Or shining Coals, that Quicken and excite:
These are the Soul or essence of Delight,   10
Ingredients or Materials of pure Bliss,
Inestimable Oyl or Wind, like His,
Who fils the World with an Eternal Being
That is an Act of Lov esteeming seeing
Upholding and Enjoying evry Being.   15
The Matter of the Soul is Power, the form
Som times a Chaos, a Night, somtimes a Storm
Som times an Univers as great as this
Somtimes an Ocean or a deep Abyss
Som times a Heaven sometimes a living Hell   20
Where Joys or Sorrows in the Abstract Dwell.
If they hit right, no Paradice can be

Affections, emotions, motions of the soul

A sweeter Region of Felicitie
Affections are the Soul when formd, and shew
25   Like those fair fruits which in that Soyl should grow.
They are the End the Glory and the Cream
The last of Gods Attainments the Supreme
And perfect Work or Being which he made
So soon producd yet that so soon may fade
30   All which depending on our Liberty
Truly our own, while they are his, may be.

                    2
The World was made, he gave us glorious Laws,
He made his Image: for what Glorious Cause?
What was the Cause that moved him to make?
35   What was the End for whose most Glorious sake?
Why doth he still support and beautify
Enrich the Earth and rule the Spacious Skie?
What moves him to come down, to send his Son
To furnish Heaven with Joys, as he hath done?
40   His Love, His Great Affection is the Cause
And ours the end of all his Works and Laws.
He loves to be our sole and whole Delight
Becaus his Goodness is most infinite.
His Goodness loveth to communicate
45   It self; and therefore he did all Create.
According to the greatness of its Measure
It loves to make it self a Sacred Treasure
To its Enjoyers, and doth take delight
Even in it self, no less then infinit
50   For being such a Treasure unto all
Whom out of Nought, it to the throne doth call.
Love being the great Cause of all alone
No other End could well propose but one
And that is Love. Love is a thing so pure
55   So Bright so Sweet so fit still to endure
It could not covet ought beside; pure Love
Aspires to nothing els, for nought doth move

But this, to be Belovd: All its content
Is there, there only is its Element.
A Goodness like it self it loves to see   60
Affected with that Goodness loves to be
And in a true Affection only finds
That which can satisfy eternal Minds.
Prize, burn with Love, Prais, laud, Admire.
Contemplat, ravishd be, griev strive desire   65
All Passions and Affections exercise
And scatter odours all the Way, as thou dost rise.
See what a Fountain of Delights he is
Oh what a Spring of Love a Spring of Bliss.
How much he gives how much he thee doth prize   70
How much himself for thee doth sacrifice
All his Endeavors sanctified by Love
Do with his Passions thy Enjoyments prove.
Lov sanctifies all Passions: O returne
His Treasures all, consume in Lov and burn   75
Be unto him what he is unto Thee.
A Spring a fountain of felicitie.
Love him as much as he loves thee. His lov
A greater Object Cause and End doth prove!
Enflaming thine, O love thy God far more   80
Then he doth Thee. Love so as to adore
O Love his Love, Griev Hope and fear for this
His Love and Goodness love if not his Bliss.

3

The World was made to be a Scene of Love,
And all the Earth a Theatre doth prove   85
Of those Affections, which we ought like Wise
Obligd and Holy men to exercise.
The Object is amazing in its Height
Of Beauty Greatness Goodness and Delight
All Wisdom Glory Majesty and Power: 90
Heaven and Earth are but a litle Bower,
Wher in he somtimes condescends to Sport:

Eternitie is his Celestial Court.
An Omnipresent Vastness doth surround
95   His Majesty, which is without all Bound.
Sweetness and Ardor, Zeal and Violence,
Excess of Lov, joynd with an Excellence
So great, might justly ravish and Enflame
Us, while his Glory only doth the same.
100   What shall we say to endless Benefits
And Obligations which no Bound admits
Exceeding Fancy Limit Term and Measure
And overflowing with all Kind of Pleasure.
He Woes, he grievs, he Fears, he doth lament
105   He hopes he covets and is discontent
My God! what are we that thou so shouldst strive
To retrive Mortals, Sinners to revive!
Canst thou upon the Throne of Glory sit
And in thy Blessedness a Thought admit
110   Of such vile Creatures! Well, my Soul, may we
Aspire to Him and his Felicitie.
Contemplat O my Soul Eternal Glory,
And with the Eys of faith behold the Story.
Griev that thou canst not with a lively Sence
115   See feel and measure so much Excellence
Fear to persist in an Offence. Desire
Hope, Covet, Languish, flie, persue, admire
Open thy chaste extended Armes, prepare
Thy Heart with Jealousy and Zeal and Care
120   Love like a Spring doth all the Passions move
And that which sanctifes them all is Love.
Lov is the only Weight of Souls, the Glue
Or sacred Cement making one of two.
His Beauty whom I lov's my only Pleasure
125   His Sacred Person is my only Treasure.
His Peace and Joy is my Felicitie
In him alone is found another I
My Hope and Fear and Care and Grief and Joy
Them selvs about my Object do employ

He quickens all my Pow'rs, and is my Life,   130
While all the Creatures are at a great Strife
Who most should honor me. My Great Desires
And Hopes are Kindled only at his fires.
Theyr dead to all things els and ought to be
Only alive to their felicitie.   135
And that is God, who doth my Lov regard
And that is God, who doth my Lov reward.

Selections from the Lambeth Manuscript

The first work in the Lambeth Manuscript, *Inducements to Retiredness*, considers the importance of solitude for persons seeking a devout life, especially clergy. It is a thoughtful work set out in meditations each ending in a poetic 'resolve', or concluding poem, modelled on the Psalms. *A Sober View* is a long theological treatise that follows one of the hottest debates of Traherne's day – the Calvinist/Arminian concern with the importance of free will. The next work, known simply as *Love*, is a beautiful untitled fragment concerning earthly and heavenly love. The shortest work in the manuscript, I believe it is nevertheless one of the most remarkable and will prove popular with readers. *Seeds of Eternity* is a short treatise whose theme is that, by the greatness of the soul, the human is made capable of union with God. *The Kingdom of God*, the final work in the manuscript, is the longest and most highly developed of the five works. It discusses the beauty of God's kingdom here on earth over 42 chapters and contains frequent references to natural philosophy and the new sciences as well as many poems. For this anthology I have selected an extract from *Love* and one long poem and two short prose pieces from *The Kingdom of God*.

Love (extracted from folios 126r–127r)

It is a prodigious thing to contemplate the illimited sweetness of Tyrannical Love. Even here upon Earth it hath been seen somtimes so transcendent and endless, that a Majestie admired and adored by others, a Beauty scarce permitted to be seen afar off, desired by
5   thousands, but by none to be familiarly approached not to be spoken to by the greatest Kings but upon the Knee, nor accosted but with

Trembling, hath surrendered up it self to be devoured by the Love
of one, and as greedily desired his Embraces as prodigaly bestowed
her own. As if they were somthing more then celestial, a favourable
Glance, a Sigh, a Touch, are able to enflame a loving Soul with   10
Raptures, and inspire Delights which no Ravishments in the World
can equal. All the Conversation is Extasie {:} feasts, Banquets,
Victories, Triumphs, Crowns, Scepters, Jewels, Perfumes, Elixars,
Spices, Treasures, Palaces, Temples, Pictures, Caresses, Songs, Musick,
whatever can be thought of; all are nothing, compared to the   15
Conversation the Lov and the Beauty of such a particular Person.
What is the reason of all this high and Strange Esteem? It is Lov
alone. This Lovly Empress hath conceived an Affection in her soul
to such a person: and the most high and worthy souls are capable of
the most high and violent Affections. This makes her Object so   20
happy and glorious in the conquest of such a rare and invincible
Potentate. And in all this the Communicativ Humor of his love is
delighted. But this is not all. As He is more enjoyable here then in
other places, he has more to enjoy. His Eys are the Sun that enlighten
her Soul, his Face is the Abridgement of heaven in her Esteem, his   25
Arms the circle of felicitie, his Breath more Sweet then Arabian Airs,
his soul a mysterious Abyss of Glory, his Accents more delightfull
then the Musick of the Spheres, his Existence the Lustre of the
World, and his person more pleaseing then the same: She livs only
for his sake, he is the only Life of all her Comforts, the Soul nay the   30
very Idol of her Soul. Thus it happeneth often in profane Loves. But
(as we said) this is not all. There is an Avaricious humor likwise in
Lov that desires to be satisfied: and to this she yeelds up herself a
willing sacrifice. He passeth through all her Guards, is reverenced by
her Nobles, enters her Closet, ransacks her Letters, Treasures, Jewels;   35
ascends her Throne, playes with her Scepter, invades her Crown,
reigns in her Kingdom; enjoys all her Gardens, Palaces, Revenues,
nay her Beauties, Desires, Affections. Her Arms, her Heart, is open
to him; and all these are esteemed only delightfull and glorious for
his sake, because he alone is the truly Beloved, the Idol of her Soul,   40
and her very Soul. Were she able to do Millions of things more for
him, she would: her very Eys and Hands are his, as well as her Jewels.
Such Fancies and Descriptions have I seen in Playes and vain

Romances. And these are sufficient to shew the Interest of being
45   Beloved. A Lover desires to be beloved: that he might be always near
and always pleasing; that he might reign in her Territories but
especialy in her Soul: all her Subjects are commanded to honor and
obey him as herself: and his Life is continued, in her desires at least,
for 1000 Ages. Flesh and Blood carries us to sensible Objects and to
50   Sensual Loves: but Reason to Objects more Divine and Powerfull.
     Let us ascend from temporal to Eternall Loves. If these Petite
and finit Lovers can be thus ardent, and by meer Instinct
understand their Interest: If they desire Beauty for these ends, and
to make themselvs more amiable, wash, perfume, and powder, and
55   curle; appear in Gay Attires, Embroyderies, Jewels, &., learn to
Sing, Dance, play on the Lute, leap, ride the great horse, shew feats
of Activitie Prowess and Chivalrie, display their Magazines of
Treasure, multiply and adorn their Attendants, expose the Glory
of their Relations to the Ey, boast their Nobilitie and descent,
60   wish for Kingdoms, or vaster Empires, acquire all kind of Graces,
practice all sorts of virtues, study all Arts of Learning, and
especialy shew an infinit unquenchable Love; and all this to appear
more Lovely, because the first and grand designe of Love is to be
beloved: what may we think of God Almighty? By how much the
65   more he loves, by so much the more doth he exceed in all.

The Kingdom of God

A Wise Man

1

A Wise Man will apply his Mind
To Joys of evry Kind:
A Good Man will take care to please
His GOD in evry thing;
5   A Holy Man can find no ease,
Untill he duly bring
His Heart to that Estate, that he might be
As Spotless even as the Deitie:

2

A Righteous Man will duly Prize
      The sun, the Stars, the Skies,   10
The Earth, the Seas, the Clouds, the Rain
      The Mountains, and the Hills,
And evry Spring that back again
      From all those Hills distills,
The Thunders, Lightenings, Meteors, Hail & Snow   15
With evry thing in Heaven or Earth below.

3

A Man that hath a Tender Sence
      Feels all the Excellence
Of evry Creature, & doth see
      In evry Kind of thing   20
Vast Treasures of felicitie
      Giv'n him by the King.
A pious man adores the Lord of Glory
A Learned Man with Joy doth read his Story.

4

A Gratefull person offers praise   25
      For all his Works & Ways,
And for the Glory which he sees
      In the Bright Heavens abov:
For all the Flowers & fruitfull Trees,
      That do express his Love   30
A Blessed Man is full of Appetites,
And in the Glory of his God delights.

5

A Heavenly person is Divine
      And like the Sun doth Shine
On all the Stars, on evry Spire   35
      Of Grass, on evry Sand;
All Lands & Ages doth admire

And doth in evry Land
Love all the persons like an Angel, which
Like Angels are, & do that Land enrich.

6

An Activ Man is Still employd:
Till all things are enjoyd
He never Rests · And then his Rest
Is in felicitie:
His Life & Business is exprest
In Joy & Melodie.
A Glorious person lives & dies in Love,
And Love his only Happiness doth prove.

7

A Wise, A good, a Holy Man,
To end where we began;
A lively, Righteous, Gratefull Soul,
A pious Learned Wight
A Blessed Man that doth controul
The Powers of the Night,
An Activ Heavenly Glorious Person is
Employd, & Busy, in the Work of Bliss.

8

He feels, he sees, he tastes, he knows,
He like his Maker grows.
He loves, & prizes all his Works
Even as his God doth doe,
And Ponders oft what Glory lurks
In all things he doth view.
While evry thing enflames his soul with love;
And evry thing his Joy, his Bliss, doth prove.

Wight, living being, creature

9

His Noble Sence exalteth all   65
    That is before his Ey,
And by their Heavenly Names doth call
    Them while on Earth they lie.
And evry thing (tho that is strange)
    Is ev'n without a Change   70
Divine to him as he himself: for he
Is Holiness, & all Felicitie.

10

The Coal which touchd the Prophet's lips
    Is hid in Simple chips:
In evry Bush he sees a fire   75
    In evry Rock a Spring,
To quench the Thirst of his Desire,
    His God in evry thing.
All Heaven descends, environs, enters him;
He is Transfigurd to a Seraphim: 80

11

Being transformd, himself he is
    A very Spring of Bliss.
And evry thing he sees, his Ey
    Doth Bless & Magnifie.
His touch whatever it doth feel,   85
    Be it or Stone, or Steel,
Or Wood, or Earth, it turns it all to Gold;
His Fingers pierce, whatever thing they hold.

Line 73, *the Coal*, see Isaiah 6.6–8; Line 75, *burning bush*, see Exodus 3.1–6; Line 76, *Rock/Spring*, see Exodus 17.1–6.

12

Like fire that alters evry thing
On which it passes, he
Doth to his own Blest Nature bring
The objects he doth see;
They also burn, & turn to fire,
Love, Pleasure, and Desire.
Joy, Praise, Peace, Gratitude, & Bliss,
When well digested, every Creature is.

13

A Glorious Region of Delights,
A Blessed Sphere of Sights
A fair transparent Mine of Treasures
A Real Map of Bliss
A fertile Womb of Heavenly Pleasures
An Ocean, or Abyss
Of Joys; a World of Glory is the place,
Wherin in Evry thing he sees his Face.

14

Tho Common, Constant, freely given,
Tho neer, tho daily seen,
Tho necessary, nay & even
Eternal, Lov, (that Queen
Of Bliss) doth for these Causes more
Esteem them, & adore
The Donor more: He takes far more Delight
That sees them with a Beatifick Sight.

15

Natures Corruption he doth hate
Seeking his former State,
Or rather, that Exalted one,

digested, matured or perfected by the action of heat, assimilated

Which truly is Divine,
To be enjoyd, when on the Throne
Of Glory he doth shine.
Where all his Body shall be purified
Flesh turnd to sense, & sense be DEIFIED.   120

The Fly (extracted from folios 289v–290v)

The Creation of Insects affords us a Clear Mirror of Almighty
Power, and Infinit Wisdom with a prospect likewise of
Transcendent Goodness. Had but one of those curious and High
stomachd Flies, been created, whose Burnisht, & Resplendent
Bodies are like Orient Gold, or Polisht Steel; whose Wings are so   5
strong, & whose Head so crownd with an Imperial Tuff, which we
often see Enthroned upon a Leaf, having a pavement of living
Emrauld beneath its feet, there contemplating all the World, That
very flie being made alone the spectator, & enjoyer of the
Universe had been a little, but sensible, King of Heaven & Earth.   10
Had some Angel or pure Intelligence, been created to consider
him, doubtless he would hav been amazed at the Height of his
estate. For all the labours of the Heavens terminate in him, He
being the only sensible that was made to Enjoy them. The very
Heavens had been, but a Canopie to the Insect, & the Earth its   15
footstool; the Sun, & Moon, & Stars its Attendants, the Seas, &
Springs, & Rivers its Refreshments, & all the Trees, & Fruits, &
flowers its Repasts, & Pleasures. There being none other living
Creature, that is corporeal, but he, as he had been the Centre, so
had he been the End of the Material World: and perhaps would   20
have seemed worthy of that Advancement. The Infinit
Workmanship about his Body, the Marvellous Consistence of his
Lims, the most neat & exquisit Distinction of his Joynts, the
Subtile & Imperceptible Ducture of his Nerves, & Endowments
of his Tongue, & Ears, & Eys, & Nostrils; the stupendious Union   25

Orient, radiant, lustrous

of his Soul, & Body, the exact & curious Symmetry of all his parts,
the feeling of his feet, & the swiftness of his Wings, the vivacity of
his Quick & Active Power, the vigor of his Resentments, his
Passions, & Affections, his Inclinations, & Principles, the
30 Imaginations of his Brain, & the Motions of his Heart, would
make him seem a Treasure wherin all Wonders were shut up
together, & that God had done as much in little there, as he had
done at large in the whole World.

The Celestial Stranger
(extracted from folios 258r–261r)

Had a Man been allwayes, in one of the Stars, or confined to the
Body of the flaming Sun, or surrounded with nothing but pure
Æther, at vast and prodigious Distances from the Earth,
acquainted with nothing but the Azure Skie, and face of Heaven,
5 litle could he Dream of any Treasures hidden in that Azure vail
afar off. Or think the earth (which perhaps would be invisible to
him, or seem but a needle's point, or Sparkle of Light) in any
measure capable of such a World of Mysteries as are
comprehended in it. Should he be let down on a suddain, & see
10 the sea, & the effects of those Influences he never Dreamd of; such
Strange Kind of Creatures; such Mysteries & Varieties; such
distinct Curiosities; such never heard of colors; such a New &
Lively Green in the Meadows; such Odoriferous & fragrant
Flowers; such Reviving, & Refreshing Winds, such Innumerable
15 Millions of unexpected Motions; such Lovely, Delicate, & Shady
Trees; so many Brisk, & Beautifull, & melodious Birds; such fluent
Springs, & Silver Streams; such Lions & Leopards, & fourefooted
Beasts; such innumerable Companies, & Hosts of Insects; such an
Ocean of fishes, Whales & Syrens, surprizing him in the Sea; such
20 Kidneys of Wheat in the fat & abundant Valleys; such Quarries of
Stones, & so Many Mines & Mettals in the Hills: such fruits &
spices; such Robes & Attires; so many Kinds of Gems, &
P[r]ecious Stones; such Cities, & Villages; such Multitude of Boyes

& Girles in the streets; such Men, such Beautifull Women upon
Earth; such Intelligent and Sagacious Spirits; such High and   25
Heavenly Minds; such Divine, & all commanding Souls; such a
Gradual Ascent from Sands to Spires of Grass, from Grass to
Insects, from these to Birds, from Birds to Beasts, from Beasts to
Men, from Earth to Heaven: such Dominion over the living
Creatures; such Combinations of States, & Common Wealths;   30
such Kingdoms & Ages; such Bookes & Universities; such
Colleges & Libraries; Such Trades & Studies; such Occupations &
Professions; such Retirements & Devotions; such Altars &
Temples; such Holy Days, & Sabbaths; such vows & prayers, such
Joys & Pleasures; such solemnities, songs, & Praises; such Sabbaths,   35
Holy Days, Sermons, Sacraments, & Ministers; such Histories and
Recordes; such Arts & Sciences; such Oracles & Miracles; such
prophesies & visions; such virtues & Graces; such sufferings &
persecutions; such Deaths and Martyrdoms; such Lov and fidelity;
such Faith, & Hope, & Desire; such obligations, such Lawes, such   40
Duties & Examples; such Rewards & Punishments; He would
think himself faln into the Paradice of God, a Phœnix nest, a Bed
of Spices, a Kingdom of Glory... It would make him cry out
How Blessed are thy Holy people, how Divine, how highly
Exalted! Heaven it self is under their feet!... The Earth seems to   45
swell with Pride, that it bears them; all its Treasure laugh & sing to
serv them: The Creatures here sacrifice their essences, & perish to
support them; the flowers are Ambitious to pleas them; The Sun
& all the stars dance attendance to them: I wonderd what made
them all to run so continualy about: And it was, that here they   50
might hav Nights and Days, & Delights in both. Verily this star is
a nest of Angels! And far more Beautiful on the Inside, then its
Splendor promised! More rich in its Contents then could hav
been conceived! Blessed are this people; Blessed in the City, &
Blessed in the field; Blessed in the seed of their Body, & in the   55
fruit of their Ground in the Increas of their Cattel, & their flocks
of Sheep: in the Increas of their kine, in their Basket & Store: They
are allwayes Blessed when they goe out, and when they come
in... They hav eaten, & are full; they have built Goodly Houses,
& Dwell therin; Their Herds & their Flocks are Multiplied, there   60

is no end of their Silver & Gold. They are conceived with
Pleasure, & come forth of the Womb to Innumerable Blessings;
They are dandled in their Infancy upon the knees of Ladies, & are
the Delights of their parents; Their Fathers and Mothers minister
65 unto them, they are embraced with kisses, & satisfyed with Loves;
They drink Honey & Nectar from their Lips in Childhood, and
grow up to greater enjoyments; The Eys of Heaven are upon them
from one end of the yeer unto the other, & the Lord himself hath
delight in them; when they sport, when they prais, when they are
70 full of pleasure, when they eat it is sweet, it is pleasant when they
drink, when they sleep it is sweet unto them: How Rich are they
to each other, how Divine and p[r]ecious in all their Wayes! The
precious Sons of Zion, comparable to fine Gold; their Teeth are as
pearl, their Eys as Diamonds; Her Nazarites were purer than the
75 snow, they were whiter than Milk, more Ruddy in Body than
Rubies, their polishing was of Saphire, Their lips like a threed of
scarlet, their Speech is Comely, their Temples like a piece of
Pomgranate within their Locks; Honey & Milk are under their
Tongue, and the smell of their Garments like that of Lebanon.
80 Their Dancings & their Feasts, their Coronations are Delightfull;
their Caresses & Marriages are sweet, & Joyfull; Their Amities &
friendships, their Contemplations & Studies, all are Divine, in a
Lively Disguise; they are Angelical... This litle Star so wide & so
full of Mysteries! So capacious, & so full of Territories, containing
85 innumerable Repositories of Delight, when we draw neer! Who
would have expected, who could hav hoped for such enjoyments?

   Thus would a Celestial Stranger be entertained in the World,
& to this voyce we ought to reecho, Blessed is the Man whom
thou chusest, & causest to approach unto thee.

Further Reading

A. M. Allchin (1989), *Landscapes of Glory* (London: DLT).

A. M. Allchin, Anne Ridler and Julia Smith (1989), *Profitable Wonders: Aspects of Thomas Traherne* (London: The Amate Press).

T. O. Beachcroft (1930), 'Traherne and the Cambridge Platonists', *Dublin Review* 186, pp. 278–90.

D. Chambers (1989), *Commentaries of Heaven: The Poems* (Salzburg, Austria: Institüt für Anglistick und Amerikanistik, Universität Salzburg).

A. L. Clements (1969), *The Mystical Poetry of Thomas Traherne* (Cambridge: Harvard University Press).

Malcolm Day (1982), *Thomas Traherne* (Boston: Twayne Publishers).

Leigh DeNeef (1988), *Traherne in Dialogue: Heidegger, Lacan, and Derrida* (Durham and London: Duke University Press).

Graham Dowell (1990), *Enjoying the World: The Rediscovery of Thomas Traherne* (London: Mowbray).

Patrick Grant (1974), *The Transformation of Sin: Studies in Donne, Herbert, Vaughan and Traherne* (Amherst: University of Massachusetts Press).

George Guffey and Carol Marks (1968), *Christian Ethicks* (Ithaca, New York: Cornell University Press).

Carol Marks (1966), 'Thomas Traherne and Cambridge Platonism', *Publications of the Modern Language Association of America*, 81, pp. 521–34.

Anne Ridler (1966), *Traherne: Poems, Centuries and Three Thanksgivings* (London: Oxford University Press).

David Scott (2001), *Sacred Tongues: The Golden Age of Spiritual Writing* (London: SPCK).

Julia Smith (ed.) (1997), 'The Ceremonial Law', *P.N. Review* 25:2, pp. 22–28.

Julia Smith (1997), *Thomas Traherne: Select Meditations* (Manchester: Carcanet).

Stanley Stewart (1970), *The Expanded Voice: The Art of Thomas Traherne* (San Marino, Huntingdon Library).

Gladys Wade (1944), *Thomas Traherne* (Princeton: Princeton University Press).